HEALING THE WOUNDED

The Costly Love of Church Discipline

JOHN WHITE & KEN BLUE

Foreword by
Ray C. Stedman

INTERVARSITY PRESS
DOWNERS GROVE, ILLINOIS 60515

InterVarsity Press is the book-publishing division of Inter-Varsity Christian Fellowship, a student movement active on campus at hundreds of universities, colleges and schools of nursing. For information about local and regional activities, write IVCF, 233 Langdon St., Madison, WI 53703.

Distributed in Canada through InterVarsity Press, 860 Denison St., Unit 3, Markham, Ontario L3R 4H1, Canada.

Cover realization: Roberta Polfus

The appendix, "Binding and Loosing" by John Howard Yoder, is reproduced from Concern: A Pamphlet Series for Questions of Christian Renewal, No. 14, 1967. Used by permission.

Portions of Robert Culp, "In Search of a Better Way," Leadership, Summer 1983, are used by permission.

ISBN 0-87784-939-0

Printed in the United States of America

Library of Congress Cataloging in Publication Data
White, John, 1924 Mar. 5-
   Healing the wounded.

   Bibliography: p.
   1. Church discipline.   I. Blue, Ken, 1945-
II. Title.
BV4520.W46 1985   262.9   85-2358
ISBN 0-87784-939-0

17	16	15	14	13	12	11	10	9	8	7	6	5	4	3	2	1
99	98	97	96	95	94	93	92	91	90	89	88	87	86	85		

To Patti

Foreword

When the apostle John wrote his account of the last words of Jesus in the upper room, he highlighted a different event than did Matthew, Mark or Luke. They focused on the Last Supper. But John featured the washing of the disciples' feet (Jn 13).

After Jesus had resumed his seat, he said to the disciples with studied impressiveness, "If I then, your Lord and Teacher, have washed your feet, you also ought to wash one another's feet." His words to Peter show he did not mean to institute a mere foot-washing ritual: "If I do not wash you, you have no part with me."

Peter instantly understood that something more than unwashed feet was involved. With characteristic impetuosity he cried, "Lord, not my feet only but also my hands and my head." The symbolic meaning of this event is made clear in Jesus' reply, "He who has bathed does not need to wash, except for his feet, but he is clean all over." Later he added, "If you know these things, blessed are you if you do them."

These words charge us with a responsibility to help keep each other's daily walk clean. What have we lost when we fail to obey them? We lose a sense of Jesus' companionship (a "part with me") and reap an impaired relationship with one another ("you also ought to wash one another's feet"). Failure to observe loving and biblical discipline (discipling?) toward one another results in weakness in our worship and strife in the body.

Fortunately, it still remains true, "When the enemy comes in like a flood the Spirit of the Lord will raise up a standard against him." God's people are discovering again the increased vitality and the loving relationships that careful biblical discipline produces. I have seen this myself. The church everywhere should welcome with deep gratitude the careful, thorough and splendidly biblical study of church discipline which John White and Ken Blue offer. It is, by far, the best I have ever seen. Its spirit is loving and sensitive, yet it reflects a painstaking scholarship supported by practical and up-to-date case studies. Everyone confronted by the need to humbly wash a brother's or sister's dirty feet will be helped by it.

Ray C. Stedman

Preface

This book was born as we shared our concerns about the church. Several times we discovered our ideas were leapfrogging whenever we discussed church discipline. Later Ken carried out research at Regent College, Vancouver, and both of us did field research, discussing our findings.

The thrust of the book concerns what we call *corrective* church discipline, church discipline's distasteful side. Corrective church discipline would heal the wounded more and be less distasteful if all of us had a broader understanding of discipline—its value and purpose. Corrective discipline begins to make sense in the larger context.

Some readers may be disappointed that having raised the broader issue we have not pursued it further or explored its application more thoroughly. To have done so would have lengthened greatly a book that is already long. The topic demands a book to itself. And while corrective discipline alone will not put the church to rights, it represents the most immediate need.

Because church discipline has potential for abuse, the authors and the publisher do not by this book pretend to offer legal advice. Nor do we encourage the denial of a church member's legal rights. Christians undertaking church discipline should first seek legal and pastoral advice about the implications of any actions they contemplate or any statements they may make. Actions and words have legal effects. We the authors encourage further study of materials we have quoted and of biblical principles within the context of specific problems. Examples of such problems in this book are fictionalized accounts so that any similarity to true-life situations are unintended by the authors and are purely coincidental.

One other problem that has arisen in writing this book (as it has already in this preface) is that of "voice." Should *we* mean Ken Blue and John White? If so, how would it be distinguished from "we Christians," or "we human beings"? Since John did the actual writing, consulting Ken all along the way, we decided John should use the first person where he gives personal illustrations, and name Ken where he was involved. We have tried to make it clear from the context when *we* means "we the authors" or "we Christians."

It is no longer possible to deny the need for the healing power of church discipline. An appalling picture is slowly emerging of a church crippled and compromised by every form of sin. Many remedies have been tried and have failed. The time has come for all Christians to exercise the costly love of corrective church discipline, restoring it to the place Christ gave it.

Part I
The Problem

1
What Is Church Discipline?

SCENARIO 1. A PASTOR WAS DISCOVERED to be lining his pockets from the church's missionary funds. A group of worried church members tackled him about the matter. But the pastor was smart. He called an emergency board meeting and had the group struck from the church membership roll for "divisiveness."

Denominational leaders came from the headquarters essentially to smooth feathers. They proposed to solve the problem by building the dismissed group a new church building. The group rejected the solution. A new building seemed to them to be a mere moral sidestep.

The pastor continued to preach and to pray from his original pulpit for a while. Then he was appointed to a position of greater prestige in a parachurch organization.

Scenario 2. A church with a rather rigid position on church discipline asked Rita, a twenty-four-year-old nurse, to "meet with the leadership about some issues in her life." She had an idea of what she was in for since the old rules on worldliness were being revived. A couple of her friends had already been "disciplined." We have only her version of the story. The leadership did not wish to be interviewed.

Although the leadership consisted of eight couples who sat round a table with her, only three of the men did any talking. The rest only sneaked occasional glances at Rita, but spent the rest of the time staring at the table or the wall while three spokesmen interrogated her. They were concerned about her light blue car and her television. A car was one thing, but *light blue*?

She felt confused, frightened and guilty. They told her to wait outside the room while they discussed her case. When she returned the chairman of the group told her that she would have to leave the church. She was worldly and needed church discipline.

Scenario 3. The assistant pastor (married) was having an affair with the seminary intern, spicing up the gossip in a large Baptist church. It enlivened the vapid triviality which members had come to take for granted as the essence of church life.

Nobody had actually caught the gossip-worthy pair in bed (in fact there is considerable doubt as to whether the affair was ever discussed with them), but the couple behaved toward each other in a deliciously indiscrete manner. Church weather became distinctly duller the day she returned to seminary.

But more excitement was in store. On completing her studies, the seminarian applied for a position on the church staff. The board met to discuss her application. One board member raised the matter of the notorious "affair," but his concerns were dismissed indignantly as prudish. She was hired.

Scenarios of this sort could be multiplied endlessly. We shall supply many. Do biblical ways of dealing with them exist? What is church discipline about? Has it a place in the contemporary church scene? If so, what is that place?

Learning to Swim Well
Discipline is training. Christian discipline is achieved by training

in godliness. Godliness is not merely a matter of being zapped by the Holy Spirit. Spiritual experiences, crises, moments of revelation all have their place. But their effects will not last unless godly training equips Christians with moral stamina.

I learned to swim by having a beautiful experience. At the shallow end of the pool I saw a coin wavering on the tiled floor. I was chest-deep in water. Grabbing the coin meant immersing my whole body in water. Under the water I couldn't see too well, but after a few tries I was successful. But I picked up something more valuable than a coin.

I found I couldn't keep my feet on the bottom. Each time I was getting low enough to grope, my feet would lose touch with the floor and start to rise. At first this was disconcerting. But suddenly it dawned on me that *I had begun to float.* Once I could maintain a little tranquility I found my face was still under the water, but that the back of my head and my shoulders were on the surface. My body was hanging in watery space, freed from the bonds of gravity like that of an astronaut. It was a glorious moment. That morning I swam from one side of the pool to the other without touching the bottom once.

My experience was valid. I really did float. My floating was not imaginary. I had learned to trust the water to uphold me. My experience was also transforming. I entered the pool as a defeated struggler. I left it a swimmer.

But my experience, while making me a real swimmer, did not make me a good swimmer. Rigid training and hard practice were needed. I even had moments of further illumination in swimming, breakthroughs in which I experienced a new freedom in the water. Most of them came during the process of training. Without the training none of them would have given me my present ability in the water.

What holds true for swimmers and swimming also holds true for Christians and godly living. Biblical knowledge and spiritual breakthroughs are not enough. Godliness also demands training. And when we use the term *Christian discipline* (or *discipline*) it is this sort of training we are talking about.

I never learned to swim the crawl properly, however, until I prevailed upon a gruff YMCA instructor to take me in hand. Once he had me in the water he seemed to forget the respect due to a middle-aged professor. He hollered. He yelled. "Reach *down!* No, not like that. Reach right down with that left arm. . . . Come on! Let your upper body roll . . . *and quit bending those knees!*"

He would make me do the same thing again. And again. And again. He kept after me when my lungs were heaving and my muscles quivering. But he had sized me up pretty well. The process took several weeks during which I had to practice daily on my own. He would praise me from time to time, and finally he was satisfied.

Who trains Christians? In theory the Holy Spirit does. But clearly we cannot blame the Holy Spirit for the lack of trained Christians nor for the pathetic moral corruption of many Christians in the church. So who trains Christians? Some people are big on one-on-one discipleship, disciplers discipling disciples. This is excellent though rare.

Most discerning Christians know the church is not what it should be. So we tackle its weakness with a patchwork of Band-Aid solutions. We organize conferences and special-emphasis weeks. We hire parachurch organizations that teach special skills, like training in personal evangelism and in Bible study methods. We add pastoral counselors to our church staff. What we fail to recognize is that the remedy must lie in grassroots, local church training or discipline. In the last chapter we shall examine how the process can get started. But first we must make sure it is worth starting.

For while God has given different gifts, the most basic training he gives is meant to come from fellow Christians in everyday encounters. *Church discipline* is the training *of* the church *by* the church. Trained professionals have their place, but they cannot and never were meant to be a substitute for the whole body.

Paul exhorts not the leadership but the *general membership* of the Thessalonian church to "admonish the idlers, encourage the fainthearted, help the weak, be patient with them all" (1 Thess 5:14). As members of the Christian community, each was to accept responsibility for the spiritual health of the others.

The idea of church discipline in many minds is confined to what one might call catastrophe discipline, discipline that waits until something goes wrong. The failure of discipline as it is often practiced can be explained in part because we are installing smoke alarms after the fire has started. It's not that extreme discipline for serious sin never works. It is just that it would work a lot better if it were part of a whole, if it were one component in ongoing training.

You may object that many churches devote a great deal of time and energy to training young Christians in discipleship. This is true. But this training, however valuable, is not the same thing we are describing by the expression "the training in godliness *of* the church *by* the church." For one thing Paul's instruction involves all the members of the church in an ongoing process, and does not just concern the young converts in time-limited instruction. With such programs you may get a certificate when you are through. With ongoing training you get your certificate in glory.

This sort of discipleship training for new Christians is often content-oriented training, instruction in Bible, in doctrine and in other practical issues. Even when the training is outside the classroom, it consists of practical training in, for example, evangelism (imparting the *content* of the gospel and the *content* of how to urge folk to believe it). But content-oriented didactic instruction was not what my YMCA instructor was giving me from the side of the pool. He was monitoring my behavior, a very different matter.

The two kinds of training are complementary. But content-oriented instruction alone will not make Christians holy. And without ongoing training in godly behavior, catastrophe discipline is likely to be fruitless.

Church discipline is anything the body of Christ does to train Christians in holiness, calling them to follow their Lord more closely. There is a special (and unpopular) category of training we call *corrective church discipline*. And corrective church discipline forms the theme of our book.

But questions arise from what I have written. If Christians were to be trained in the way I was taught to swim the crawl, could not the training be expected to do away with, or to minimize the need for, corrective church discipline, that ugly, embarrassing, inconvenient kind? When people are in training surely their mistakes are caught at once. In that case there should be no hassles over adultery, theft or drunkenness.

Do any churches exist where training in holiness forms the fabric of church life? They are rare, but they exist. Their membership, vigorous and growing, is drawn largely from unchurched working classes. And certainly the training they give is loving yet rigorous.

Does the training eliminate or minimize the need for corrective discipline? One can only judge by what takes place. In these churches corrective discipline tends in fact to occur more frequently than in mainline churches. Godly training does not eliminate the need for corrective church discipline. Rather it forms the context in which corrective discipline can most helpfully take place. For in most churches corrective discipline is avoided because it is incongruous with the tenor of church life and incompatible with its hidden agenda.

We would love to develop the broad theme of discipline. It is a glorious theme that could be a current of fresh and heavenly air blowing away the staleness enervating our churches. It is the whole of which corrective church discipline is but a part, essential both for the understanding and the practice of corrective discipline. But corrective discipline is the real and necessary question we address.

It has to be. We cannot wait for radical changes in churches before we deal with sin. Sin flourishes among us, clamoring for correction. And though we recognize that corrective discipline is but first aid for the wounds of an indisciplined church, we must tackle it first.

"The secular world is almost wholly unimpressed by the Church today," writes John Stott. "There is widespread departure from Christian moral standards. So long as the Church tolerates sin in itself and does not judge itself . . . and fails to manifest visibly the power of Jesus Christ to save from sin, it will never attract the world to Christ."[1] Stott is right. In spite of renewals and revivals, the world remains unimpressed. Church discipline that takes sin seriously is almost extinct (especially in traditional churches) and church morality is often tarnished. Many younger Christians have little idea what corrective church discipline is and have little interest in it. People under forty do not flock to hear addresses on it. The topic registers a blank in their minds. People over forty prefer not to think about it.

The Dangers of Corrective Discipline

Why is corrective church discipline so widely neglected? It is found in the Scriptures. It is found in church history. What has happened? Many reasons account for its decline. The first must be that of its abuses. Harsh and misguided church discipline in the past has made Christian leaders and older Christians back off.

From its earliest years the church has fluctuated between leniency and severity, alternating between malicious ingenuity in nailing offenders to irresponsibility in turning a blind eye to their sins. John McNeill writes:

St. Gregory the Wonder-Worker, bishop of Neo-Caesarea in Pontus, about A.D. 260, . . . indicates four grades or classes of penitents prior to their restoration to full communion. The "weepers" or "mourners" stand outside the door of the church, beseeching the faithful to intercede for them; the "hearers" are placed in the narthex (a passage between the door and the nave); the "kneelers" kneel within the nave amid the standing congregation; the "co-standers" join normally in the service with others except that they may not take communion.[2]

As time went on the system grew more complex and more severe. The Council of Ancyra grappled with the problem of Christians who had weakened under persecution and denied their Lord. For them the discipline consisted of "one year as hearers, three year as kneelers, and two years as co-standers."[3] Later still, St. Basil of Caesarea in letters between A.D. 374-376 prescribed for the sin of adultery a total of fifteen years of discipline, four with the weepers, five with the hearers, four with the kneelers and two with the standers.

Sitting comfortably in our armchairs we find it easy to recognize the absurdity of such measures. Yet equally inappropriate measures still occur, and there is no guarantee that excesses will not take place.

In the seventeenth century John Owen wrote, "Discipline hath been metamorphosed into a hideous monster, an engine of ... domination and tyranny, for ... the terror of the souls of men, and the destruction of their lives with all their earthly concern, unto the erection of a tyrannical empire."[4]

Discipline can be an ugly word. Charles Dickens' novels describe the unjust discipline inflicted on the poor and the weak in Victorian England and in revolutionary France. Solzhenitsyn describes similar oppression in Russia. And while we call such measures oppressive, the political leaders of those places and times saw them as necessary for the preservation of society.

Our era is no more enlightened. There are boys' boarding schools where students tremble at the thought of vicious measures carried out in the name of discipline, prisons in many lands where political prisoners are reduced to quivering imbeciles before they are permitted to die. We live in an age of technically advanced barbarity.

And the church is not immune. This is the age of Jonestown and deprogramming. Corrective discipline is dangerous because some people, even Christian people, have a "need" to control others. We must not be naive about the horrendous possibilities. The victims of corrective church discipline cry out from the pages of church history. The same dangers will threaten more victims if it is reintroduced. We must look the dangers in the eye before opting for it.

Some years ago the Pennsylvania public was appalled by a TV magazine featuring an outbreak of church discipline in a small group of rural churches. Over fifty members had been "shunned" or excommunicated. Most shunned members fell into one of two groups—people over sixty and young people under twenty-five. Church officials refused to comment. The program focused mainly on the plight of a group of feeble senior citizens who had been turned out of a nursing home because they owned television sets (a sign of worldliness). The old people would gladly have relinquished the sets, but indicated that the quality of their repentance had not satisfied the church authorities.

At all times and in all places leaders (both religious as well as governmental) have seen discipline as serving valuable social functions, the creation of order instead of chaos, of predictability in the place of confusion. We might say that discipline, however cruel, may be the lesser of two evils. In its most tyrannical forms it is probably better than anarchy. Freedom is impossible without some form of discipline. And since few of us are capable of perfect self-discipline, some form of external persuasion is called for if we are to know a free and effective society.

But the abuses of discipline, rather than discipline itself, are what we must fear. Is there anything good that isn't abused? How about marriage? Or surgery? Ought we to abandon them because of their abuses? Law is abused. Should we therefore opt for chaos? The only reason why there are not more abuses of corrective church discipline is simple: there isn't enough practiced for many abuses to occur.

Yes, the reintroduction of corrective church discipline will bring dangers with it. Some people may get badly hurt. *But the dangers of failing to restore it will be incalculably greater.*

Four Aims

Sometimes corrective church discipline has been practiced and practiced well. Where it has failed, it has failed because God's people have been too narrow in their understanding. They have perceived two aims, and two aims only for it: the purity of the church and the restoration of the sinner to righteousness.[5] Both are important.

But it seems to us that two even more important principles have been neglected, both of them arising out of the very heart of the gospel: reconciliation and freedom. Sin brings alienation, alienation from God and alienation among brothers and sisters. Christ died and rose that we might be reconciled to God and to one another. Church discipline must aim at reconciliation among brethren.

Christ also died to set us free, free from bondage, and free both from guilt and from feelings of guilt. Christians are to be set free from the fear of criticisms by their fellow Christians. We were meant to fear God and sin alone. Corrective discipline when properly carried out should set us free from every fear save the fear of God and the fear of sin. In part two on the aims of church discipline, we shall devote a chapter to each of these four concerns: reconciliation, church purity, restoration of sinners and freedom.

A church community where no fears exist save those of God and sin would be unusual. In practice the creation of such a loving, caring community should be the starting place of our reintroduction to corrective discipline. For church discipline needs a soil to take root in and a climate to foster its growth. It can only flourish in a community where people not only know one another extremely well, but where they trust and love one another enough to level with one another.

In a large church it is impossible for everyone to know everyone else intimately. It is also impossible to trust and to love people you don't know well. Therefore, whatever a church's ecclesiology, that church must make provision for the kind of intimate fellowship where members can share, encourage, exhort and pray for one another lovingly, trustingly. We plan to look more closely at the problems hindering such a fellowship in part three where we look at the practical side of corrective church discipline.

The Cost

Christ warns us against building towers without counting the cost. Already we have mentioned that corrective church discipline has in the past been abandoned because of its abuses. We have also stated that its reintroduction could be accompanied by mistakes, mistakes causing spiritual damage rather than spiritual help. We don't usually do something perfectly the first time. But there are two other factors we must mention before we proceed. The first is an issue that is fundamental to all forms of discipline.

Discipline appears to be based on force. After all, didn't my swimming instructor at the Y *make* me do things, pushing me beyond my feeble limits? Or did he? When I think about it I can only do so with gratitude. After all, I twisted *his* arm first.

What actually happened is that the two of us recognized we had parallel goals. I wanted to swim the crawl well, wanted it so badly that I didn't care what it cost me. He wanted to teach me properly. And I knew he was not hollering at me out of malice or to humiliate me. Nor was it that I particularly wanted to please him. I wanted *to do it right*.

We had entered without even thinking about the matter into an unspoken covenant: he to train and I to be trained. I suppose if he had suspected I wasn't responding to him with tremendous effort (he got no extra pay), he could have said, "Look, let's forget it, huh? You're really not interested in what I have to offer." But I wanted to learn, and I trusted the guy. I nearly killed myself, knowing he was giving me exactly what I both wanted and needed.

The ultimate step in church discipline, sometimes called excommunication, is the ultimate step of what looks like coercion. It is the church's way of saying, "Let's forget it, huh? You're really not interested in what we have to offer. If you were, you'd be following instructions more—or at least be trying to. If you want to try again sometime, though, come back and we'll talk about it." And at that point you would leave the fellowship, hopefully for only a temporary period.

But because discipline is a two-way contract, I can also choose to end the relationship. I can voluntarily remove myself from the church's authority just as I can voluntarily put myself under it. The church does not force me to. But if I want what the church has to offer (as I wanted to learn to swim), I will endure its discipline. Likewise, churches need to realize that they cannot exercise discipline without the cooperation of the one being disciplined. They cannot force anyone to do anything. Realizing this, plus re-emphasizing the aims of reconciliation and freedom, provides the antidote to abuses of discipline.

The second factor is the cost of love. Church discipline is costly because my brother's and my sister's business become my business. In a sense I am their spiritual keeper, just as they are mine. If they are sick, I am called to pour the healing arts of the Holy Spirit into their souls. I do not show love by ignoring a fellow

Christian in spiritual pain. No. I respond. As church members we are accountable for one another's well being. This places a responsibility on me to encourage, admonish, praise, exercise patience and even to rebuke (not merely to pray, and certainly not to gossip). It also means I must be open to exhortations addressed to me. I thus become less of a private person than I would be otherwise.

How far should such a principle be taken? How much of myself ought I to reveal? To what extent should we be concerned with the details of one another's lives? Do other people have the right to tell me what to do? Do I have the right to tell them? What authority does the church have over our private lives?

Everything depends on how we look at matters. How badly does the church as a whole need to be holy? How much do we want to become godly?

I wanted to swim the crawl. I wanted it badly enough to put up with what to someone looking on might have seemed like bullying, humiliation and sadism. It didn't feel that way to me. I was only too glad to pay the price to get what I wanted. And my delight was transformed into gratitude as the ease and flow of a fluid crawl slowly became mine.

How badly do you want to live a godly life?

2

Barriers
to Church
Discipline

IN COUNTING THE COST OF CORRECTIVE church discipline we
began to see the reasons why it is practiced so little. Let us
consider several in detail. Other fears may plague us, but these at
least should be considered at the outset.

A Limited View
We tend to fail to see corrective church discipline in the larger
context of general church discipline. We forget its broad function
of mutual training in godly living. Training is where discipline
starts.

Jesus *trained* his disciples or, if you like, he *disciplined* them. He
did not entertain them with special musical numbers. He lived
with them, ate with them, shared their sleeping and living
quarters. He knew them intimately. They probably heard him
preach the same sermons many times (sermons so packed with

content that they needed repeated hearings).

He also gave them private tutorials. He sent them on mission assignments. He chose them, exposed his own life to them, leveled with them, warned them, prayed over them. He allowed himself to be crucified before their terrified gaze; he then rose and revealed himself to them. He reproved their fears and unbelief with the utmost gentleness—and then sent them out to conquer the world.

Likewise, when we train God's people, we cannot limit ourselves to weekly sermons, prayer meetings and occasional mission conferences or evangelistic outreaches. Training in godliness must be full orbed. As Paul wrote the Thessalonians, "We were ready to share with you not only the gospel of God but also our own selves" (1 Thess 2:8). Our whole life needs to be on view and available to those we wish to follow Christ more closely.

Individualism and Criticism
A second barrier is that we are blinded by our own culture's prejudices and fears. Some years ago a group of New Tribes missionaries were engaged in the difficult, delicate and dangerous task of making contact with a primitive tribe in the Bolivian jungle. Soon after the initial meeting, at a point where two groups of fearful men, the missionaries and the tribesmen, were tentatively trying to communicate, one missionary plucked a pen from his pocket to write down the sounds one of the naked tribesmen was making. At once the natives fled. Their world was a world of magic and demons. They had never seen a pen. Who was to know what terrible power it might contain? They shared a world view common to the culture that had molded them, a world view that would seem nonsensical to us.

On the other hand, our world view would seem nonsensical (however frightening and impressive) to them. We like to think that our beliefs about the world are not only biblical but logical and reasonable. We have little idea of the extent to which we are molded by the culture we live in. When we tour foreign countries we are inclined not only to admire but also to pity and to criticize, forgetting all the time that we wear invisible spectacles, the spectacles of the culture by which our own values have been shaped.

We are brainwashed by Western thinking. Those of us reared in the Western world, particularly those of us reared in North America, have been programmed to behave as individualists. Older civilizations were more inclined to think of themselves as integral parts of units. Their values were different. The group was more important to them than it is to us.

The late Thom Hopler tells the story:

When I first held tryouts in Kenya for a track meet, I could not get the students to compete against each other. They said, "We will select the one who is the fastest runner. He will run against the other school." I asked, "Why?" They said, "If we pick the one who can run best for us, then we can all cheer him on to victory against the other school. But we could never cheer him on to victory if he had selected himself by his own qualities. If we compete against ourselves, we will divide ourselves, and we will not be able to compete against the other school." That's corporateness. That is the way a tribal society operates.[1]

It may surprise us that Kenyan values correspond more closely to biblical values than do our own. Old Testament judgments did not only fall on individuals but on peoples. Israel and Judah were judged as nations. Righteous Jews went into captivity along with rebellious and wicked Jews when the nation was taken to Babylon.

We are unaware of our different slant on life, taking it for granted as the norm. So in our churches as well as in clubs and societies we have instinctive feelings about minding our own business and not interfering in other people's affairs. But these ways are merely cultural, not superior.

We are products of Western culture. One key value Western culture has implanted in us is individualism. We stand on our own feet, mind our own business and get mad when someone threatens to take away our liberty. We live and let live. Our concept of freedom, even our Christian thinking about freedom, arises from Western individualism. It does not arise from Scripture.

Our individualism (as well as our sinfulness) militates against exercising corrective church discipline. To be members of the people of God means that our physical and spiritual well-being becomes our brother's business and his well-being becomes ours. But such attitudes are so alien to the Western church that when we do opt for biblical discipline, we will be criticized. John Stott comments:

> There are many reasons advanced against the enforcement of stricter discipline. The modern quest for the unity of the church; the hatred of all intolerance (which fails to distinguish between a right intolerance of sin and a wrong intolerance of spirit); a mistaken notion that such public discipline betokens pride, animosity or priggishness; a horror of anything approaching the public accusation meetings promoted by communist governments; a misinterpretation of the parable of the wheat and tares as prohibiting all attempts to separate the bad from the good in the visible church; a fear of public scandal in these days of mass media of communication—these and other arguments are used to hinder the restoration of a proper discipline to the church.[2]

Daniel Wray concurs, "Today the church faces a moral crisis within her own ranks. Her failure to take a strong stand against evil (even in her own midst), and her tendency to be more concerned about what is expedient than what is right, have robbed the church of biblical integrity and power."[3]

Churches which exercise corrective discipline might, however unjustly, be called cults. This could have serious consequences in a day when governments are more inclined to feel responsible for dealing with aberrant religious groups. The U.S. Supreme Court upholds the principle of freedom of religion, but has never taken it upon itself to give a comprehensive definition of the term *religion*. Church discipline could be seen as discriminatory and as a violation of individual rights, both in Canada and in the United States. In a recent court case, a jury in Tulsa awarded $390,000 to a woman who was accused of fornication by her church and later removed from fellowship.[4] But we must not let ourselves be scared away from church discipline whatever the political or financial consequences might be. Churches have always brought criticism down on their heads during the periods of their greatest faithfulness.

Preaching, Power and Holiness

Corrective church discipline is also thwarted by the belief that Spirit-inspired preaching of Scripture will by itself produce holy congregations. Congregations can wallow comfortably in familiar rhetoric while hearts are hardened to the Spirit's pleading. The same seed that produces a full ear of grain may also produce feeble, fruitless, weed-choked green shoots.

We may organize revivals, special meetings, have renewal experiences, concentrate on the knowledge of Scripture. But the church will experience only temporary (though genuine) changes. (The Word is powerful but some of us run away from it.) Demons sit silently and comfortably among the congregation, and their Master will sow his own seed. It will grow and flourish because we are looking for some easier answer than the way of obedience, in this case obedience to Christ's commands to exercise corrective church discipline.

Knowledge may increase while pride abounds. Spiritual gifts may be lavishly poured out and freely exercised while incest is tolerated (1 Cor 5). The Devil is able to produce his own signs and wonders, so that even Spirit-produced signs and wonders may not hold the world's attention for long. Only God can produce holiness. And God has ordained a means whereby the congregation may experience ongoing cleansing. It is not episodic revival. It is the church dealing with sin through discipline.

Fear of Exposure, Fear of Confrontation

Fourth, corrective church discipline is rare because we so fear honestly confessing our sins to others. How many of us hide skeletons that rattle restlessly inside us at the possibility of exposure? Could habits, shames and bondages become known by others?

Let us be clear about one thing before proceeding further. Jesus did not make us detectives to ferret out one another's secret flaws. Rather, as we shall see later, it was to provide a forgiving and understanding community where we may find pardon, healing and strength.

It is not easy to admit failures and weaknesses to our fellow Christians, but it becomes easier when we discover our brothers and sisters are vulnerable and needy, and can therefore be understanding. Yet how can churches become communities of this sort? Clearly leadership will be needed if such a quality of Christian fellowship is to develop. But from whence will the leadership come?

A moving testimony from a conference speaker and pornography addict was featured anonymously in a 1982 issue of *Leadership*.[5] It told of an agony healed, but also confirmed what many of us already know, that sexual sin is common even among pastors and Christian leaders. And how can discipline begin if it does not begin there?

Another barrier is our fear of confronting others with possible wrongdoing. It is not easy to talk to someone about their sin. It will become easier if we get into the habit of encouraging and gently exhorting our fellow believers. But the step from encouragement to exhortation is nothing compared to the step from exhortation to confrontation and rebuke. Who wants to confront a brother or sister with his or her personal sin? Yet must the holiness of God's people be thwarted by our cowardliness and our red faces? We need to be convinced of the rightness of doing this sort of thing and then know the Holy Spirit's aid in carrying out our duty. We shall say more about this in part three.

Change and the Calloused Conscience
The next barrier is tradition and the fear of change. We may be too rough on the Pharisees. Their zeal for God's Word exceeded our own. In their generation they stood like a bastion against the liberalism of the Sadducees. Yet they overemphasized parts of Scripture and neglected others. They also added their own traditions to Scripture. And in both of these respects we are like them. Often we cling to certain traditions in our churches because of the psychological security we unconsciously derive from them. They make us feel comfortable.

Change is a threat and radical change is terrifying. Our fear about church discipline is akin to the fear Jesus awoke in the scribes and Pharisees by what seemed to them a radical departure from their traditions. For like us they naively supposed that all their traditions were Yahweh's will. Our fears are understandable, but we must face them for what they are. And Christ will come to our aid if we are willing to admit their true nature.

Our lack of sensitivity to the horrors of sin is a further roadblock. We resist the idea of dealing with sin in others because our consciences have been dulled if not seared. We are selective about sins Scripture mentions. We hold in contempt those Christians who struggle against homosexuality (though not all struggle, of course) while cheerfully ignoring sins like living for money and material possessions. We tolerate pride and gossip, and have no idea how to cope with dishonesty.

Ken Blue learned of a church in Dallas facing a severe embarrassment. A prominent member was bankrupt and had fallen into the practice of double-billing his clients. Or that was the story going round the church. And it had the church worried.

"Sounds like a classic case for going and talking to the brother as in Matthew 18," Ken commented to Michael, a friend of his.

"But it's not a *moral* sin," Michael replied. It quickly became evident that *moral* meant sexual to Michael. And apparently church discipline only applied to sexual sin.

Nothing could be further from the truth. "There are six things which the LORD hates, seven which are an abomination to him: haughty eyes, a lying tongue, and hands that shed innocent blood, a heart that devises wicked plans, feet that make haste to run to evil, a false witness who breathes out lies, and a man who sows discord among brothers" (Prov 6:16-19). Sexual sin does not appear on the list. Pride and lying come first. Even divisiveness figures on it. This is not to say that sexual sin is unimportant. But we make the point at the outset because we do not wish to give the idea that sexual sin is more important than it actually is. This impression might be picked up from the frequency with which sexual sin appears in this book. This frequency reflects *the frequency with which sexual sin occurs among Christians* rather than its special importance to God.

We shall not get into complex ethical issues, or attempt to offer a hierarchy of sins. But let there be no doubt at the outset that sin is sin is sin.

Our consciences are blunted from overexposure. The sight of a dead body has a profound effect on most of us. But medical students who dissect human corpses grow callous and careless within a week of starting their dissections. And in the same way we have all become deadened to the appalling nature of sin.

Because our consciences have been dulled we are not gripped by the urgency for the church to discipline sin. We are fooled by our material prosperity, our lovely sanctuaries, our large congregations and our growing social prestige. Meanwhile sin stalks through our congregations laughing as it inflicts devastating casualties in our ranks. We never see these casualties since not only have our consciences been dulled, but our eyes are looking in wrong directions.

The Shrinking Army
The last barrier is the idea that corrective church discipline will thin our ranks. In fact, the opposite is occurring. The ranks of our combat troops are shrinking without corrective church discipline. Notice please, we are talking about combat troops not merely about people whose names are on church membership rolls. Corrective church discipline will not cause churches to shrink. It will cause them to grow, not only numerically but in combat power.

People are attracted to churches where real discipline exists. But the real irony is that we have assumed that growing church membership means that the ranks of the Christian army are growing whereas the number of combat troops is in fact shrinking. Churches have become hospitals where sin-sick souls are given aspirin and entertainment to distract them from the diseases of their souls. God forgive us, we are more concerned with numbers than with holiness.

The church's growth is largely a cancerous growth, and we do not even know it.

3

Jesus
and
Power

I SAY TO MY DOG, "SIT!" and he sits. I have authority, and I use it.
I exercise power. My dog's happiness will depend very much on
the sort of person I am—weak, strong, kind, cruel or some mixture
of these. Who I am will determine how I see my dog and how I
exercise my authority and power.

Earlier we discussed coercion in relation to church discipline
without saying anything about authority and power. But now we
must do so, since these are also involved.

We have already made it clear that any coercive element in
church discipline must be benign. It must be a grassroots
phenomenon and one that permeates the whole fabric of the
church. This might suggest that ideal church discipline would do
away with leadership in the church, just as Marxism is supposed
to do away with centralized government. Yet God uses human
leadership. In the Bible human leaders alternately exercised and

abused both authority and power. Church history excites us as we follow the epic struggles between the valiant Davids and the evil Goliaths of the church. Therefore we must not be ostriches with issues like authority and power. Neither must we let ourselves be torn, trapped and bewildered in a bramble-ridden forest of abstract concepts. Throughout this book we hope to focus more on leaders than on leadership, and on how authority and power are exercised more than on what exactly they are. But we must at least attempt to define our terms.

Authority and power are like husbands and wives in modern society. Ideally they should live together, but in practice they often don't. If you have authority, you have the *right* to do something. Society may have given you that right, either by electing you or investing you in some sort of office. Power, on the other hand, gives you an *ability* to control. And if your control is over people, you can make them do things they do not want to do. We intend to focus on the moral dimension of both power and authority. We shall look briefly at the lives of sinners and of one sinless person in their exercise of authority and power.

The Authority Wielder

All licit authority comes from God. Any authority that is not God-given is usurped or *il*licit. Having stated the general principle we shall unblushingly sidestep some intriguing and controversial questions it raises, at least for the moment. After all, Jesus did. So we too shall say, "Render to authorities what belongs to them and to God what belongs to him," and leave it there. This book is about church discipline. While we may be forced to do a little more thinking on the topic of Caesar vis-à-vis God, it will have to wait for the present. Rather we ask the question, How does God use his authority and power? And as a partial answer we shall look at God-made-flesh. We shall ask how Jesus handled authority and power, and how he and the apostles recommend that we do so.

The Son of man could claim supreme authority. On many occasions he demonstrated it. His preaching and teaching had the ring of authority. Following the Sermon on the Mount, "the crowds were astonished at his teaching, for he taught them as one who had authority, and not as their scribes" (Mt 7:28-29). He also commanded the attention and respect of those he spoke to. In the synagogue in Capernaum where his teaching was accompanied by a demonstration of power, the people cried, "What is this? A new teaching! With authority he commands even the unclean spirits, and they obey him" (Mk 1:27). His fame spread at once.

The reaction of the crowd was significant. Jewish rabbis cast demons out. They practiced exorcism using the Sacred Name (for money). But their exorcistic rituals were time consuming. As they watched Jesus, the crowds at once spotted a difference. Jesus *commanded.* He exercised authority, and demons promptly obeyed. So his listeners ascribed the same authority to his teaching that demons recognized in his orders.

We could call his teaching power-authenticated or God-authenticated. Such teaching will carry conviction. The teacher's person will be invested with authority, whatever his official capacity. Paul claimed that his own preaching was of this sort. It was not "in plausible words of wisdom, but in demonstration of the Spirit and of power" (1 Cor 2:4).

Supreme Authority

Some people might argue that Christ's authority was analogous to the authority we attribute to mediums and weather forecasters. He impressed people so that they gave him authority, attributing to him a power that he would not otherwise have had. It arose, as it were, spontaneously in the minds of his listeners.

Undoubtedly he benefited from the support of the multitude. "By what authority are you doing these things, and who gave you this authority?" the chief priests demanded. Christ spurned their questions. Instead he forced them to face their own cowardice. "The baptism of John, whence was it?" he asked. "From heaven or from men?" The chief priests knew a political trap when they saw one and foxily evaded committing themselves. "We do not know" (Mt 21:23-27).

Yet Christ's authority lay in far more than political astuteness and mass appeal. He referred to Satan as "the ruler of this world" and rightly asserted, "He has no power over me" (Jn 14:30). James

Kallas may oversimplify the mystery of God's sovereignty and human suffering, but he is right in seeing Christ's earthly advent as a power clash. A greater rule demonstrated its power over a lesser to announce the final doom of Satan.[1]

Not only as God, but as the Son of man, Jesus penetrated a hostile kingdom in coming to earth. But since "the ruler of this world" ruled by the power of evil, and since there was no shred of evil in Jesus the man, Satan could have no power over him. Holiness clothed him as armor. The Spirit of holiness radiated from him in searing, irresistible authority.

There was and is no limit to his authority. Yet how did he exercise it? Do we find him abusing it? Did he press his advantage to crush the political power of his adversaries? Apart from an occasional stern rebuke, when did he ever treat his disciples with anything but tenderness, courtesy and respect?

"You know that the rulers of the Gentiles lord it over them," he once observed to his disciples, "and their great men exercise authority over them. It shall not be so among you; but whoever would be great among you must be your servant, and whoever would be first among you must be your slave; even as the Son of man came not to be served but to serve, and to give his life as a ransom for many" (Mt 20:25-28).

He was the Teacher. The Lord. Knowing his death was but hours away he acknowledged he was both. "You call me Teacher and Lord; *and you are right, for so I am*" (Jn 13:13). Yet how did he demonstrate his authority? He did so by giving the word a new content. Authority and power were to be used meekly to enhance the purity and comfort of others. Not as a histrionic gesture but in a genuinely prophetic demonstration he took on the role of a slave. He washed the feet of eleven disciples and one traitor (Jn 13:3-20).

This dramatic action is consistent with his words and actions throughout his public career. From its outset, as he stood with sinners awaiting baptism (Lk 3:21-22), as he subsequently faced temptation by Satan (Lk 4:1-12), to his final hours, he refused to use his power and authority for personal ends. During his arrest, Peter's violence was gently rebuked with, "Put your sword back into its place. . . . Do you think that I cannot appeal to my Father, and he will at once send me more than twelve legions of angels? But how then should the scriptures be fulfilled . . . ?" (Mt 26:52-54). For all his power Jesus never lost the common touch. He displayed no power-lust. He was never bossy. His teaching required no exercise of control. Never a man taught like he.

Good leaders *produce* good leaders and bad leaders, bad ones. Hitlers and Bormanns produce SS brutes. Christ produced a Peter, who for all his impetuosity would one day write, "So I exhort the elders among you, as a fellow elder. . . . Tend the flock of God that is your charge, not by constraint but willingly, not for shameful gain but eagerly, not as domineering over those in your charge but being examples to the flock. . . . Clothe yourselves, all of you, with humility toward one another" (1 Pet 5:1-5).

Authority Abused
Yet sadly the history of corrective church discipline (or what has been carried on in the name of church discipline) has been characterized more by the abuse of authority than by the kind of authority Christ taught and exemplified. Carnal anger, arrogance, even brutality and murder stain the pages of church history.

Christ's power came from heaven. Some church leaders delight to remember it and hail themselves as its channels. But remember that Satan's lack of power and control over Jesus did not lie merely in his divinity so much as in the sinlessness of his humanity. Many leaders forget that. And therefore Satan has often had power over them when they thought they were acting in the name of Christ. Satan has had his way among God's people because sin in the lives of people and leaders alike gave him a hold he could never claim over our Master.

There is a tension among Christians that arises from what might be called a *high view of the church* and a *high view of Scripture*. Both have their dangers. The first emphasizes the authority of the church over the lives of God's people. Similarly a high view of Scripture emphasizes the need for Scripture to control the behavior of Christians. Both emphases are found in Scripture. There is no tension between them. The tension arises in the minds of leaders who try to use either church or Bible or both to control God's people. Church leaders are themselves under the authority of Scripture, but its authority is never to be coercive: it does not make leaders into rulers.

For all his heroism and godliness, Watchman Nee, because of his high view of the church, fell into error at this point. Writing of Christ's authority, Nee stated, "Hence you [should] recognize not only the head, Christ, but also those whom God has set in the body to represent the head. If you are at odds with them you will also be at odds with God."[2] The danger lies in the last sentence: *"If you are at odds with them you will also be at odds with God."* As Barr puts it, "Nee teaches that whenever Christians disagree with their leaders, they ipso facto disagree with God."[3] The implications of Nee's teaching has throughout history been carried further than Nee might have realized. It is currently taught in some groups to infantilize and subjugate Christians to a form of "spiritual" and sometimes physical tyranny.

And the same tyranny is exercised by people with a high view of Scripture. In their case selfishness takes the form of mistaking what God is saying in Scripture for their particular brand of interpretation of Scripture.

Christian leaders, being human, can give place to sin and pride. They are not always aware when they are doing so, and have forgotten that our Master's total immunity (as the Son of man) to Satanic control arose from his sinless human walk. Human leaders who make pronouncements in the name of God or of Scripture may be unaware of the power of Satan over them at that moment. At the very least they will be making carnal statements in the name of God or of Scripture, while at worst they will be meriting the same rebuke that Jesus once gave to Peter, "Get behind me, Satan!"

The Church

We have discussed authority. We have discussed discipline. We have avoided discussing the church. Clearly we must give some explanation of what the church is. It is commonly agreed that in the New Testament only two concepts exist: that of the *churches* and that of the *church*. The former were bodies of believers in specific geographical locations, the latter the universal church, the bride of Christ made up of all believers.

Twenty centuries after the New Testament we face a more complex situation. Churches are now ubiquitous, widely varied and institutionalized. There has been the division of Eastern and Western Churches, followed many centuries later by the Reformation in the Western Church. The Reformation has been followed by increasing fragmentation of churches and church organizations, a fragmentation exported all over the world (often unintentionally and along with the good news itself) by the modern missionary movement.

The reaction among some Christian groups has been to look toward a renewal of unity. This demands more rigorous thinking and theologizing about the church and new attempts to formulate a mutually satisfactory ecclesiology. But the practice of corrective church discipline does not demand, and cannot wait for, an adequate ecclesiology. For a start to be made it is only necessary to recognize first that the body of Christ must be expressed at least in some local and visible form and, second, that churches and church organizations should recognize one another's existence and relate with mutual respect. We need not even wait for the second of these two. Where respect already exists we must make use of it. Where it does not exist we should strive for it.

We already have local churches and church organizations. We need and have leaders. They may not meet our ideals, but they are all we have.

Church leaders need our prayers. Like all of us they must be accountable to God and to the bodies of which they form a part. As Jerram Barrs puts it in another context, "We must recognize human fallibility. Sin may affect the functioning of any gift."[4]

Leaders are meant to be facilitators not despots. Their role is essential. But they must use their authority in the way Jesus did. And they must never forget that while (like all of us) they have a line to heaven, unlike Jesus they are open to the wiles of the devil. Such leaders are needed to guide God's people along the disciplined road of freedom.

Part II

The Goals of Corrective Church Discipline

4
The Ministry of Reconciliation

SOME MARRIED PEOPLE SAY it's worth having a good fight for the fun of making up again. We might not all agree, but many of us have experienced the warmth and the sweetness of a genuine reconciliation following a quarrel. And Christians who have experienced the sweetness of reconciliation following corrective church discipline are quick to agree that this has its own sweetness.

Disagreements among close friends are painful. Vipers of resentment and bitterness bite deeply when we hug them to us. And sadly, we can throw the vipers away without being healed. Some people opt for a forgetting. They refuse to let their lives be ruined by resentment. Bitterness gives place to alienation. The old relationship is sealed behind a stone door.

But the solution is never ideal. If reconciliation is possible it is infinitely better. Reconciliation brings growth as well as restoring something too precious to seal behind stone. But pseudoreconciliation will not do.

"Bob and Rose are back together again," a gossiper remarks.

"For how long this time, I wonder?" comes the cynical rejoinder.

True reconciliation never takes place without change in the parties involved. And reconciliation, true and costly reconciliation, lies at the heart of the gospel, a gospel Paul calls "the ministry of reconciliation." What is the gospel about if not reconciliation? "All this [our being a new creation] is from God, who through Christ reconciled us to himself and gave us the ministry of reconciliation; that is, in Christ God was reconciling the world to himself . . . and entrusting to us the message of reconciliation. So we are ambassadors for Christ. . . . We beseech you on behalf of Christ, be reconciled to God" (2 Cor 5:18-20).

In this chapter we have several goals. First, we want to define reconciliation, showing how it lies at the heart of the gospel. Second, we want to show that it is the most basic of the four aims of corrective church discipline (the other three being church purity, restoration and freedom, each of which will be discussed in turn in the next three chapters). Third, we want to demonstrate that if reconciliation is our primary aim in corrective church discipline, we will be protected from cruel excesses. We conclude by briefly discussing the costs and the benefits of following the biblical pattern of correction.

War and Peace

Is reconciliation at the heart of the gospel? "Any theology which is faithful to the Church of Jesus Christ . . . cannot but be a theology of reconciliation, for reconciliation belongs to the essential nature and mission of the Church in the world," writes Tom Torrance.[1] Reconciliation means replacing a state of war with one of peace. Whereas hostility and alienation separate, reconciliation restores harmony and closeness.

We are at war. We are each at war within ourselves. We are also at war with one another, and ultimately, we are at war with God. The breakdown began at the dawn of our history when we sinned and fell.

Reconciliation is that process by which hostility is abolished and peace restored. It is God replacing war with peace, alienation with friendship and intimacy.

But let us re-emphasize that the alienation is multidirectional. When Adam lost his peace with God, he lost his peace with himself. When Eve sinned she lost both her internal peace and her closeness to her husband. As we shall see later, this holds true throughout biblical history. Peace with God, peace with ourselves and peace with our neighbors (even peace with our physical environment) are inseparably linked. To lose one is to lose all. To regain *the* one (peace with God) is to begin to regain all.

The story of God's dealings with the nation Israel is the story of a God who wished to dwell in the midst of a people. So he devised means to do so without compromising his holiness. He exercised patience and long-suffering over his people's rebellions and idolatry, mourning them and predicting a time when his rage would be appeased, his righteous demands met and his relationship with his people fully re-established.

For peace to be restored he had to deal with sin. But holiness was not in itself the end. It was a necessary condition without which God and his people could not be reconciled. The most frequently quoted words from John's Gospel do not read, "For God so hated sin, that he gave his only Son that whoever believes in him, might be made righteous." Such a statement would be true. But God is even more concerned about sinners than about sin. He loved "the world" of sinners. He is the shepherd desperate over one lost sheep, the woman searching for her lost silver coin, and the father wildly delirious over the return of his erring boy (Lk 15:1-32).

The gospel is the story of a loving God reaching out to people. Paul, as God's servant, tells us he preaches the gospel because love forces him to (2 Cor 5:14). Love, he tells us, reconciles us to God (2 Cor 5:18). Indeed if God reconciled us to himself while we were shaking our fists at him, how much more, having been reconciled, will he treat us with mercy now? (Rom 5:9-11).

Such love makes our salvation more than ransom from merited punishment. Something has happened to us. We have been given hearts that instinctively cry, "Abba"—"my very own dear father!" (Rom 8:15; Gal 4:6). God tells us, "I will be a father to you, and you shall be my sons and daughters" (2 Cor 6:18). We receive "the full rights of sons" (Gal 4:5 NIV).

Such is God's mercy. And so great is the love he bears us that he has "raised us up with him, and made us sit with him in the heavenly places in Christ Jesus, that in the coming ages he might show the immeasurable riches of his grace in kindness toward us" (Eph 2:6-7).

Once "far off," we "have been brought near in the blood of Christ. *For he is our peace*" (Eph 2:13-14). Christ preached peace to us, his enemies, so that instead of being estranged from him we might become members of his very household (Eph 2:17-19).

Need we quote more Scripture to demonstrate that reconciliation is what the gospel is all about? That justification and redemption were but the costly means by which our restoration to peace with God was secured?

Peace in the Community of the Saints

Since sin created alienation and hostility multidirectionally (estranging us from ourselves, from one another, from God and even from our environment), it would seem logical that God's plan would reverse the process. This is precisely what Paul teaches. The verses above talk about our being members of God's household and fellow citizens with the saints. Now it would not be much good to be reconciled to a household at continual war with itself or given citizenship of a city in turmoil. Thus reconciliation is intended to restore peace among God's people.

Now if church discipline, including corrective discipline, is training in holiness, it necessarily follows that it will aim to create and maintain reconciliation among Christians. Yet the writings of two thousand years on the topic fail to show awareness of this. Ken Blue devoted months of study to a careful review of the writings of contemporary and remote theologians to discover whether there was any reference to any other aim motivating corrective church discipline other than church purity and setting sinners straight. As a result he writes: "Today as always the two values stressed in connection with discipline are the purity of the community and the individual while neglecting the health of relationships. While these two emphases witness to the church's holiness and its redeeming ministry, they do not take into account that the church is also social. The koinonia of the church is . . . not recognized sufficiently."[2]

The Short Step to Barbarism

For two thousand years corrective church discipline has been at best a partial good. It has been inadequately understood as well as imperfectly applied. And sometimes the consequences have been appalling. Can these abuses be attributed merely to the social and psychological pressures of the time? We think not. As we said earlier, it's not that people in earlier eras were less civilized than we. For we ourselves are merely technologically advanced barbarians. Even today it is so easy, so very, very easy to become cruel to one's fellow human beings even under the pretext of helping them. Christian conversion is no guarantee that one will never hurt others.

In Stanley Milgram's well-known experiment, unwitting subjects became willing to inflict what they thought were horrendous electrical tortures on students.[3] The subjects could observe the students through a one-way mirror. The students had been instructed beforehand to act out imaginary anguish whenever their indicators showed an "electric shock" was being given them, though no electricity ever reached them. The experiment was a fake. But before the beginning of the experiment the subjects had been given enthusiastic accounts of how quickly students would learn, provided they were "shocked" hard enough as soon as they made an error. Within minutes some subjects thought they were applying as much as four hundred fifty volts, unaware in the excitement of the experiment of what cruelty they might be inflicting.

Were they sadistic? No more than the rest of us. Such experiments reveal how quickly any of us could hurt our neighbors or even our family members in the name of helping them. The horror which nauseates us when we read about torture and cruelty can quickly be eroded under certain conditions. Our stomachs can quickly be inured to other people's pain, so long as we are convinced we are doing what is best.

The Inquisition, like the Holocaust, could be perpetrated by most of us under appropriate conditions. Leon Jaworski (Chief Prosecutor, Nazi War Crimes Trials and Watergate) describes in detail the brutal murder of eight U.S. airmen during World War 2.[4] Taken captive after being shot down, the men were on their way to a POW camp, when their train was stopped at Russelsheim, a small town in the state of Hesse. The railway line ahead was being repaired.

A crowd gathered to look at the Americans. Hostile murmurs began. Then as murmurs became shouts and as shouts rose to a crescendo, the men were dragged from the train to be stoned, kicked and battered. A couple of citizens approached the Protestant pastor and the Catholic priest, begging them to intervene. Neither complied.

In a brief space of time two or three unrecognizable, bloody corpses lay on the ground beside the train, while the rest lay at different points along the streets of the town. Even in death they were not left alone, the battering continuing until intestines and inner organs lay exposed to view. What amazed Jaworski was that the perpetrators of the crime were normal, kindly people.

Having made every allowance for the abnormal times, Jaworski concludes, "As I thought of Joseph Hartgen, the two sisters and the other 'good-hearted' people of Russelsheim, I realized that none of us know what we are capable of doing until we reach such a point. As we cannot envision the heights we can reach by placing ourselves in the hands of God, neither can we imagine the depths to which we can sink without him."[5] And tragically, many of us think we are acting in his name, when the psychological factors playing upon us are precisely those that affected the people of Russelsheim.

Such atrocities are not German atrocities, but *human* atrocities, and there is no race on earth and few Christian groups on earth who have not at one time or another perpetrated them. Jews may attribute them to Christians, Protestants to Catholics, but the long memory of history tells another story. Nor does "godliness" or "spirituality" make us immune from committing atrocities. The saintly Bernard of Clairvaux was part of a movement to eradicate simple, Bible-centered worship in twelfth-century France.[6]

Widespread ignorance exists among Protestant Christians about the horrendous executions of such groups as the Anabaptists during the Reformation. Zwingli, a leading Swiss reformer, felt strongly that it was the church's responsibility to guide civil authorities. Those persecutions instigated by Zwingli and his followers make church history in the sixteenth century grim reading. Broadbent writes:

> The spread of the churches in Austria and the surrounding states was marvellous; the accounts of the numbers put to death are terrible, yet there never failed men willing to take up the dangerous work of evangelists and elders. Of some it is recorded, "they went with joy to their death. While some were being drowned and put to death, the others who were waiting their turn, sang and waited with joy the death that was theirs when the executioner took them in hand. They were firm in the truth which they knew, and fortified in the faith which they had from God." Such steadfastness constantly aroused astonishment, and inquiry as to the source of their strength. Many were won by it to the faith, but by the religious leaders, both of the Roman Catholic and Reformed Churches, it was generally attributed to Satan.[7]

What sin is here being disciplined? Baptism by immersion. Zwingli had persuaded the magistrates that it was a threat to civil order. Luther likewise invoked civil authority against the Anabaptists for similar reasons.

Sin and Reconciliation

If human nature is constant, and we are all capable of abusing corrective church discipline, whether we lived a thousand years ago or yesterday, how can we guard against potential misuse in the future? By a correct understanding of Scripture. There must have been a failure in the Reformation to understand the very nature of the gospel, or at least of the implications of reconciliation. John Howard Yoder writes the following in "Binding and Loosing" (which is reproduced in its entirety in the appendix).

Any textbook discussion of "church discipline" aligns several . . . reasons for its application by the church:

☐ the purity of the church *as a valuable goal in its own right* [our italics];

☐ protecting the reputation of the church before the outside world;

☐ testifying to the righteous demands of God;

☐ dramatizing the demands of church membership, especially to new or young church members;

☐ safeguarding against the relativization and loss of common Christian and moral standards.

Real as they are as by-products and logical as they may well be in motivating the church, it is striking that these concerns are not a part of the New Testament picture. These reasonings all put the church in a posture of maintaining her own righteousness, whereas the New Testament speaks in terms of shared forgiveness.[8]

This was what the Reformation missed. Neither the purity of the church nor the restoration of sinners are ends in themselves. They are milestones on the way to the ultimate goal of ending our alienation from God and each other. Putting reconciliation first and letting it rule over the other aims of corrective discipline will protect us from using it cruelly.

The classic teaching on church discipline begins in Matthew 18:15, a passage we will consider in detail in chapter eight. Jesus is instructing the apostles in the kinds of personal relationships expected of members of his kingdom. "If your brother sins against you, go and tell him his fault, between you and him alone. If he listens to you, you have gained your brother." Some old manuscripts omit the words "against you." In a sense it hardly matters whether or not Jesus used them on that occasion. Jesus did give us, as the apostles also did, clear instructions on what to do when a brother sinned, whether that sin was directed to our personal hurt or not.

In another setting Luke quotes Jesus as saying, "Take heed to yourselves; if your brother sins, rebuke him, and if he repents, forgive him" (17:3). Paul in Galatians 6:1-2 also tells us, "Brethren, if a man is overtaken in any trespass, you who are spiritual should restore him in a spirit of gentleness. . . . Bear one another's burdens, and so fulfil the law of Christ."

Sin, as we have said so many times, always alienates. But sin that is "against us" is doubly alienating. We can pretend to be tolerant of sins that do not wound us personally. But if you spread a lying story about me, or if you "borrow" my new car (you were going to ask my permission, but I wasn't around) and smash it up in a traffic accident, the fragile balloon of my tolerance bursts.

What demands does the kingdom place upon you when your brother sins *against you*? How are you expected to behave? You are to go to him. You are to go alone. You are to go with a certain goal in mind, the goal of restoring the broken relationship. To obey Jesus will be tough. But he sets tough standards for members of his kingdom.

The last sentence in Matthew 18:15 is of inestimable importance. "If he listens to you . . ." The word Jesus uses means "heeds," "pays attention to," implying a change of heart in the brother in question. "If he listens to you, *you have gained your brother*." You have achieved the main goal of the confrontation. You have mended a broken relationship. The alienation is gone. Remember again why Jesus came to earth. What aim other than reconciliation could have been in the mind of the Teacher who himself came to win back lost sinners?

As we shall see later there is nothing automatic about the process of speaking to someone who has sinned. A great deal is involved, and many different results could follow. For now the basic point is enough. We go seeking reconciliation, not conquest, nor to assert our rights. Any attempt to correct has a specific aim: reconciliation.

Of course the sinner has to want to be reconciled, to want it badly enough to acknowledge sin and repent of it. Most of us understand this principle clearly enough when we preach the gospel to the unconverted. We fail to understand it when we think of our brothers and sisters in need of discipline. And because of our failure to understand, either we carry out corrective discipline in a wrong spirit or else, fearing the consequences, we close our minds to carrying it out at all.

What goes on between you and your brother may in fact be a long and protracted affair. He may need counsel, guidance. All this we will come to later. For now we must focus on the goal you have in mind in going to him. That goal is reconciliation, the restoration of a relationship that has been lost.

Because we fail to grasp the core of the gospel message, we misunderstand the terms we use in preaching it. We preach to "the lost," without realizing that we do not mean "the perishing." While it is true that the unconverted are perishing, Jesus had a different point to make in his parables about the lost sheep, the lost coin and the lost son (Lk 15). We tend to picture a sheep that has lost its way. Similarly we see the so-called prodigal son as a young man who has tragically missed his way in life. And all the time we miss what Jesus is trying to explain. He was responding to the scribes and the Pharisees who complained, "This man receives sinners and eats with them" (Lk 15:2). In response Christ dramatized the issue, trying to make them understand how God *feels* about sinners he has lost.

When you lose something you value, you get upset. Jesus told the scribes that God felt about sinners much as a shepherd feels about a missing sheep, a woman about her missing cash and a father about his missing boy. *Lost* in the parables means lost *by* somebody, somebody who keenly felt the loss. Each story is climaxed by delirious excitement at the restoration of whatever or whoever had been lost. The stories teach us that disrupted relationships cause God personal grief, and their restoration personal joy. "Just so, I tell you, there will be more joy in heaven over one sinner who repents than over ninety-nine righteous persons who need no repentance" (Lk 15:7).

The Joys and Perils of Intimacy

Intimacy is not all joy. Good friendships are desirable but dangerous. The delight of being close to someone is always accompanied by the peril of hurting or being hurt by that someone. Intimacy and the potential for pain go hand in hand. You cannot have one without the other. So in subtle ways we arrange our living to get the most from the community with the least hurt in a never-ending dance of advances toward and retreats from greater closeness.

The technology of urban life has made distancing easier. We can share the same television set and live eons apart. It saves us from the urgency of revealing the hurts and joys of our hearts. We can greet the caretaker or the filling-station attendant with the illusion that we know them intimately when we don't know them at all.

Yet Western society is plagued with a paradoxical yearning for intimacy, perilous though it may be. Such is the vacuum in our hearts, yes, even in our Christian hearts, that we fall ready prey to nude encounter groups, to cults and fads like the human potential movement which draw us with the promise of heart's ease and the joys of closeness.

Christian community is to restore what human society has lost through sin. But has it done so? Warmer, deeper fellowships exist among Christians. But they are not common. Who feels safe enough in the average church to open up to fellow Christians, to share the painful, shameful and even the trivial everyday things that community was meant to be all about? How would our confidences be received? With polite boredom? Dismay? Gossip? Instead we hide behind our social masks, enjoying what we can, but never being off our guard. A sociologist studying the average Christian church would see no essential difference in the quality of its human relationships and those of some local club, say a community service group or a country club.

What is "the fellowship of the saints" meant to be? *Koinonia* is the Greek word for fellowship. But it has nothing to do with "having fellowship" over a cup of coffee, even though there is no incompatibility between coffee and koinonia. Rather, it centers around such ideas as sharing, holding things in common (in the way fishermen may jointly own a boat). But there is a specific Christian content to koinonia. There are specific things we share, all of them fruits of our reconciliation with God. They are things that touch the raw depths of our souls, our deepest fears, our blackest guilts. Divine love has met us to cover our secret shame, to abolish our guilt and to remove our fears in an ongoing, forgiving and caring relationship.

But divine love places us under an obligation. Cleansing must continue. We must love as we have been loved, accept as we have been accepted, forgive as we have been forgiven. The task is not easy.

Ken Blue once counseled two sisters, both members of the same church, who had been quarreling since their childhood. When he called them together he found they had so many grievances that they hardly knew where to begin. Eventually each sister aired her complaints while Ken sat and listened. But before long the meeting degenerated into a shouting match. Ken intervened to point out that the object of the exercise, according to Jesus, was reconciliation. But reconciliation was the furthest thing from both sisters' minds.

Ken, however, knew that both sisters genuinely loved Christ and were committed to obedience. He therefore made a second approach, going to each sister privately and telling each that to refuse reconciliation with the other would be treason against their Lord. There was a second meeting where deep reconciliation was sealed. More importantly, the reconciliation has held up. Each sister's tenderness for Christ won out.

We struggle. Our faith at times wanes unaccountably. To our shame, we fall repeatedly into sin, hopefully to find renewed forgiveness and deliverance. And these experiences too are to be offered to and shared with those who are in need. To share in "the fellowship of the saints" is to belong to a reconciled and reconciling community, bound together by bonds of loving faithfulness.

5

The Holy,
Spotless
Bride

WHEN I WAS VERY YOUNG I ASKED, "Why do brides dress up in white?"

"Because white is a symbol of purity."

"Oh, I see."

But I didn't see. In fact it was a long time before I gathered what bridal purity meant. And by that time I wondered why brides continued to dress in white. I also pondered on the reasons why in those days bridegrooms dressed in gray.

Ken Blue and I have a similar feeling of unreality about the doctrine of the church's purity. We read about it in Scripture. The church was meant to wear white. Paul tells us, "Christ loved the church and gave himself up for her, that he might sanctify her, . . . that he might present the church to himself in splendor, without spot or wrinkle or any such thing, that she might be holy and without blemish" (Eph 5:25-27).

But the church is anything but pure. She would be a lot purer if corrective church discipline were revived. The pre-eminence of reconciliation in corrective discipline in no way minimizes the need for a purified church. Holiness was not a bargain-basement price for the church's reconciliation. To Christ the purity of the bride cost his Incarnation and death.

Paul's words are astounding. God turns the common standards upside-down. In this case rather than the bride it is the groom who will be robed in white and whose purity cannot be called in question. And the unsullied bridegroom chooses a strumpet for a bride. More than this he does to her something no human has ever been capable of doing to a fallen woman. He makes her clean, pure, holy.

He is still doing so. Her purity and holiness are of even greater importance to him now. It is a holy bride he will espouse. Do you suppose that her present dubious moral hygiene pleases him?

"Ah, she is not really pure. He just *sees* her as pure. She is pure *in his sight* so to speak." Or so some Bible teachers tell us. There is a certain amount of truth in what they say. But are we to suppose Jesus does not see the church's foulness? What do you suppose the seven letters at the beginning of the book of Revelation are about? Christ saw some of those churches as anything but pure. Still his attitude of passionate concern is plain.

"Yes, but you can't expect perfection in a church," a man said to me. "There'll always be sin in the church as long as the church is on earth."

Possibly so. It is not the statement itself we quarrel with but with the implications of the statement. "There will always be sin . . ." (So let's not get too upset about it.) He didn't say that, and probably he wouldn't have, but what other implication could such a statement have? We're not going to make it, so why try too hard? Obviously we can't let things go entirely to the dogs, but let's be sensible about it . . .

Sensible about *sin*?

Moderate about *holiness*?

Let us return to the argument of the previous chapter. What does Christ want? A bride pure from sin. Why? Because sin alienates. Purity is a prerequisite to reconciliation, to the union of the bride and groom.

But we made it clear that sin alienates horizontally as well as vertically. Sin brings alienation among church members. Reconciliation is more than a series of reconciliations between individuals and God. It has a social dimension. It is reconciliation between a people-made-holy and God. Purity exists where reconciliation among the members of the body exists. Where reconciliation among members of the church does not exist, the church is not holy, the bride not pure.

Why is it that the thought of a holy and godly church concerns us so little? While the church of past centuries focused too much on purity to the exclusion of the other goals of corrective discipline, we have ignored it entirely too much. As stated earlier, we have become calloused to sin. To our great shame, *holiness* has become an empty word. Can it be because we have other goals for the church, goals which supersede her holiness? Does our preoccupation with building programs, with our public image in the community, with our innovative programming or with our church growth suffocate our concern for the holiness of God's people?

We are blind. As churches we no longer see God. Only the pure in heart see him and our hearts are no longer pure. We even forget we are at war. The hosts of wickedness are doing all they can to befoul the bride of Jesus. How better could they express their hatred of him? If you are honest you will admit that at times it is hard to conceive the ferocity and the intensity of the battles in heavenly places, the heinous and implacable will of evil to destroy and to mar anything that bears the name of Jesus. And so we play church while the fires of hell rage round us. What ought we to be doing? We ought to be exercising corrective church discipline. It is a matter of life and death for the church.

When Great Fear Fell

It is not easy to understand how we can be loving, reconciling and rebuking at the same time. Nevertheless, examples of corrective church discipline involving one or two devastating rebukes may help us see the importance of church purity.

Christ's rebuke to Peter was horrendous. "Get behind me, Satan! You are a hindrance to me; for you are not on the side of God, but of men" (Mt 16:23). Whatever other implications the rebuke may have, it alerts us to the possibility that words and actions of church members may unwittingly represent Satanic opposition to the Lord of the church and his sovereign purposes.

The issue becomes plainer in the story of Ananias and Sapphira (Acts 4:32—5:11). Peter has now advanced from one rebuked to one who rebukes. The central issue in the story concerns lying and deceit. Members of the young and growing churches in Jerusalem, bursting with love and generosity, were selling their possessions and laying the proceeds at the apostles' feet to be used for the common good. There was no compulsion in the matter. The gestures were spontaneous outpourings arising from compassion for those in need. Nor did the generous donors necessarily sell all of their possessions. Barnabas simply sold a field he owned and gave the proceeds to the church. Ananias was under no compulsion to follow even this example.

It would appear that he and Sapphira wanted to get on the generosity bandwagon. But their desire was tainted by pride and deceit. They conspired to sell some land and then pretend they were giving all but retain some of the proceeds of the sale. It is the element of deceit that called for the terrible disciplinary action that followed. Consider Peter's comments. "Ananias, why has Satan filled your heart *to lie to the Holy Spirit?*" (5:3).

Evidently the deceit was more significant than it appeared on the surface. Our view might be that only the church was being deceived. But God saw the matter differently, "You have not lied to men but to God" (5:4). Of Sapphira Peter demands, "How is it that you have agreed together to tempt the Spirit of the Lord?" (5:9). And as Peter spoke his words of rebuke, the Holy Spirit confirmed his words. Each deceiver in turn fell dead at his feet.

The incident is shocking. It was shocking to the church at the time. "And great fear came upon the whole church, and upon all who heard of these things" (5:11). But the fear was a healthy fear and one which would increase the church's liberty and power.

Moreover, it was not a fear of Peter, but a fear of the power, the discernment and the holiness of God.

What we are seeing is not normative, but extraordinary church discipline. Peter was given what charismatic Christians would call a word of knowledge. He merely spoke what God was showing him and what God was doing. Having once been a passive instrument of Satan, he now becomes the instrument of the Spirit's disciplinary action—the *Holy* Spirit's disciplinary action.

It would be presumptuous folly for us to expect people to fall dead at our rebukes. But it will be worse folly to suppose that the Holy Spirit will not act in the same way in the twentieth century. He is still doing so in some areas of the world.

More importantly, we see the vast difference between God's standards of purity and our own. To us the sin of Ananias and Sapphira would seem relatively benign. God's standard remains absolute. The purity of the church is of inestimable importance to him.

John Owen seems to have been more in touch with God's standards than we are. The following words are truer now than when he first wrote them: "But it is so come to pass, that let men be never so notorious and flagitiously wicked, until they become pests of the earth, yet are they esteemed to belong to the church of Christ; and not only so, but it is considered little less than schism to forbid them communion of the church in all its sacred privileges."[1]

Church Impurity

It may be unwise to generalize about the impurity of the church since most of the impurity is under wraps. At least it is partly under wraps. Sin is impossible to hide completely.

If ever you have been in one of those small gatherings where Christians have learned to trust one another enough to open up about their struggles with sin, you probably had a mixture of reactions. You might experience relief. ("Thank God it's not just me!") And with that a rush of encouragement along with release and gratitude for the support of mutual prayer. Tears of joy, perhaps.

A second kind of reaction would be a sort of double take. After the meeting is over (the weeping, the counsel, the commitments, the prayer, the new resolves and alliances against sin) and you're driving home, then comes the question, "If two members of a group like this grapple with that kind of sin, how widespread is it among Christians generally?" I have had that same double take on numbers of occasions.

Sin will out. Our sins are known to the unchurched and especially to the cynical critics of the church. We ought to take notice of such critics more than we do. They're biased, but then who isn't? Church members most certainly are. Our critics will generally give us good clues as to where sin exists in the church, sin that needs to be dealt with with discipline. So let's listen to what our critics have to say. The quotes on each of the following topics represent a sort of collage of many statements made to us. You may have heard them yourself.

Sexual Morality. "They're just a bunch of hypocrites." (This remark might serve as a general heading or even a leitmotif of all that follows.) "They run around. They swap wives, then join a different church. Their kids do the same things our kids do. Not that that's so terrible. Only they try to make out they're so good. I guess they gotta pretend or else they're not welcome in church anymore."

True or false? The world is remarkably perceptive. It takes sinners to spot sinners. Clearly the judgment is too general. Sexual immorality is widespread among Christians, but less widespread than the world would like to believe. But who is satisfied with that standard? Most certainly the church's bridegroom is not.

Dishonesty. Here the hypocrisy theme is more heated. "The way some of them make their money. . . . I wouldn't do business with that bunch for anything. You just can't trust them." Again the judgment is too general. Honest Christians do exist and there are thoroughly honest Christian businesses. But that is beside the point. Dishonest Christian business practices are widespread, and in many cases they seem to form no impediment to church membership.

Christians lie frequently. Ken and I have to confess we find it a constant struggle to remain personally honest all day every day. But for many, dishonesty is such a habit that they seem unaware of it.

I spent several days getting to know the inner workings of the Xenos Christian Fellowship in Columbus, Ohio. Most of their adherents are converts, but a few are former members of other churches. "We don't have nearly as many problems with dishonesty in those who don't have a Christian background," the leaders told us. "They *know* they lie but are much quicker to come to terms with it. But those who come from some evangelical churches seem to have got an ingrained habit of living on two levels—the 'victorious Christian' level and a carnal level at the same time. Their inner dishonesty is deeply ingrained, and it's very hard for them to come to grips with it." Our experience tends to confirm this.

Church Cupidity. "They're not interested in us—only in our money." The word *they* seems in this case to refer indiscriminately to churches and to Christian radio and TV programs. The charge though general is difficult to deny. How can such sins be purified from the church? Here the leadership itself seems to be at fault. To whom are the Christian TV entrepreneurs accountable? Not to their public, for their public are in some cases, unfortunately, their dupes. To whom are their boards (where they exist) accountable? Where does the idea of corrective church discipline apply here?

But in our role as ordinary church members we must not pride ourselves on our *relative* respectability. Do the churches we belong to wear a mantle of cupidity? Are their boards out to create wealthy churches? If so, how ought we to deal with board members?

Christian Love. "They're supposed to love one another. How come they're always fighting? In any church you go to, after a while you always find it's *this* family against *that* family. And do they ever hate each other! Some of them never speak. And there's always the ruling clique of the ones who've been there the longest. If you're not in with the right bunch, you're a nobody."

Do you hear the muttering of embittered souls here? Are the

critics passive do-everything-for-me pew warmers? Even if they are, we cannot dismiss the criticism. Their attitude may be wrong while their opinion remains accurate. Just now we are not discussing the wrong attitude of embittered former church members, but the purity of the church. Bitter or not, their opinion may be correct, and before we embark on a crusade of mote removing, the Lord of the church might be wanting us to excise some logs from our own eyes.

These sins that our critics have noticed are not the only ones that need church discipline. They are a mere sampling that indicates that impurity in the church is noticed by the world. And we dishonor God when we fail to deal with our sins.

Purity and Reconciliation

How is church purity related to reconciliation? And how do sinful church members make us impure as a body? We have already discussed the matter in principle, but let us look at a quotation from Paul. "Your boasting is not good. Do you not know that a little leaven leavens the whole lump? Cleanse out the old leaven that you may be a new lump, as you really are unleavened. For Christ, our paschal lamb, has been sacrificed. Let us, therefore, celebrate the festival, not with the old leaven, the leaven of malice and evil, but with the unleavened bread of sincerity and truth" (1 Cor 5:6-8).

"A little leaven leavens the whole lump." Meaning what? One rotten apple makes the whole barrel rotten? Notice how Calvin interprets the verse. "The second purpose [of corrective church discipline] is that the good be not corrupted by the constant company of the wicked, as commonly happens. For (such is our tendency to wander from the way) there is nothing easier than to be led away by bad examples from moral living. The apostle noted this tendency when he bade the Corinthians expel the incestuous man from their company. 'A little leaven,' he says, 'ferments the whole lump.' "[2]

Calvin is correct when he suggests that Paul means that one sinner makes all sinful. He is also right when he tells us that bad company corrupts good behavior. But is he correct when he reads this second truth into what Paul is saying? Or has he missed the point Paul is driving at? We believe he has. How then does one practicing sinner make the whole church sinful?

The passage is quoted from a letter Paul was writing to a church that was, by some criteria, a very spiritual church, charismatic in fact—prophecy, tongues, the whole bit. Nor did Paul have any objection to this, provided the spiritual gifts were used for the benefit of the church as a whole (rather than the glory of any one individual) and that they were exercised in an orderly fashion.

If we read 1 Corinthians 5 superficially we might conclude Paul was worried about a case of incest between a church member and his father's wife. Calvin is correct in perceiving it is not the promiscuity alone that bothers Paul. What did concern him was the lack of corrective church discipline for an affair that was the talk of the church. Evidently the church felt it was doing great. Paul tells them they are inappropriately arrogant. They seem to have been not unlike some churches today whose members flatter themselves on their loving attitude toward people who sin in ways that are becoming more fashionable. No narrow, judgmental bigots, they!

So back to our original question. What is the meaning of the phrase, "a little leaven leavens the whole lump"? Paul was concerned about the Corinthians' indifference to the sin in their midst. "And you are arrogant! Ought you not rather to mourn?" (1 Cor 5:2).

From the context there is no means of being sure what Paul means by his remark about the leaven. Why then do we disagree with Calvin? Think about real-life churches for a moment. Whenever scandal becomes widely known in a church something automatically happens to its members. To know about something is to develop a stance toward it, to have fantasies, feelings and attitudes. Let us look at some common, real-life attitudes.

"Just wait till I tell Jim."

"I always did say there was something wrong with that guy."

"I bet the pastor's going to get on his high horse about this."

"I bet the pastor's going to let this slip by just like he did when . . ."

"I bet the pastor's going to give us some more sloppy stuff about 'loving acceptance'!"

"I wish people would just mind their own business!"

"That does it! I wonder who found out? Peter and I had better stop seeing each other for a bit. They'll be on to us next."

"Let's get together and pray for them."

"Let's pray that the Holy Spirit will give people a more charitable spirit toward them."

"Let's pray that *someone* will start standing up against *sin.*"

Unless someone in the church decides to go lovingly to the person involved in the scandal with the object of establishing the truth, effecting righteousness and seeking to bring about reconciliation, *every single member in the church who is aware of the situation is sinning every moment—is in fact a participator in the sin of the "identified sinner" in one way or another. The church is sinning by avoiding corrective church discipline.*

We repeat, sin corrodes fellowship multidirectionally. It therefore destroys koinonia, that fellowship which is truly fellowship in Christ. Much that goes under the name of fellowship in Christ is a mere travesty of that glorious intimacy of the reconciled and the reconcilers, the pardoned and the pardoners. And when a member breaks that fellowship by sin, and we are aware that this is so, we are abandoning a brother or sister in their sin and alienation.

Some of the attitudes above may represent what Paul refers to as "the leaven of malice and evil" (1 Cor 5:8). It is most unusual for a church to have a completely united attitude in the face of a sinning member; and while we commonly assume that the Corinthian church members unitedly shrugged their shoulders over the incident, the context does not necessarily imply this.

We believe that in this passage *leaven* symbolizes sin in general. They were doing well until they heard what was going on. But once they knew, changes began to take place in them, resentments, doubts, fears, justifications of guilts and so on. Most important among these changes were feelings about the person concerned. And they did nothing about them. They just let matters slide.

In the context of Paul's letter, love meant doing a number of things, all of which involved confronting the person concerned. And not to deal with the matter (or to procrastinate) is every bit as bad as to condone it. Both are sins. Condoning the sin represents rebellion against God and his Word. To avoid the sinner is to abandon a brother in his sin—an abandonment which is sin against God and against the brother.

These are the ways in which a little leaven leavens the whole lump, or in which one rotten apple makes the whole barrel rotten. As apples in the church-barrel we are not, and were never intended to be, individually sealed in plastic.

In chapters eight and nine we shall expound the Corinthian and Matthew passages more carefully. We shall also deal with many practical questions they raise. Our present purpose is to show that corrective church discipline does aim to promote church purity, but not in the way we commonly assume. The purification is intimately related to the aim of reconciliation. Reconciliation is the primary goal of corrective discipline, just as yearning for reconciliation is its primary motive. The yearning weeps over the progressive and sinful alienation infesting the community. A leavened church is an impure and alienated church.

The Mystery

We began this chapter by looking at Christ's motive in giving his life for the church. He wanted a pure and holy bride. "This mystery is a profound one," Paul tells us (Eph 5:32). The church is foul. We tolerate treachery, gossip, theft, sexual immorality, oppression, pride. Is there any sin in the whole world that is not both found and tolerated in the church? As Calvin put it, we are "a conspiracy of wicked and abandoned men."

Mystery? A most profound mystery! How could Christ love, die and continue to intercede for such a bride? Yet he does so. And he yearns for and pleads with her. He rebukes her and issues letters of stern warning to her. And he will make her holy as we fulfill our responsibility to exercise corrective church discipline.

6

Restoring
the
Fallen

RESTORING SINNERS IS NOT ONLY a classic aim of corrective church discipline, it is also a biblical aim. Restoration takes place when sinners are brought back to righteousness. They repent. That is, they acknowledge their sinfulness and turn from it to godly behavior. Rebels see their folly and wrongness and abandon their insurrection. The fallen realize they are in the dirt, get to their feet and brush themselves off.

Church purity is primarily concerned with the righteousness of Christ's body. Restoration, however, is primarily concerned with the righteousness of an individual. For fellowship to be re-established with a brother or sister (reconciliation), the church must be pure. And for the church to be pure, individuals must be made pure (restoration).

Restoration thus opens the door to reconciliation. The former rebel becomes a friend again. The fallen become comrades in arms with the fighters. The once wounded resume their roles as integral members of a healthy community. The goal of their reconciliation is achieved along with that of their restoration to holy living.

Thus to be restored means more than to have repented and been forgiven. Sin damages. It weakens resistance, dulls conscience, debases appetites, brutalizes instincts. It is habit-forming and character-changing. Sinners need to be healed and rehabilitated. We do not use the word *restoration* to refer to being restored to fellowship. Rather *restoration* means being brought back to the holiness one held before a fall. At best, in practice, it means something more than the narrow definition of the word would suggest—but rather becoming better, wiser and stronger. It is to such a condition that repentance must be the doorway.

Ask a Christian leader whether corrective church discipline is important and you may get a guarded yes. Ask why it is so rarely practiced and you are likely to get some reply like, "Well the whole question of church discipline is a difficult one. . . ." What it boils down to is that corrective discipline as it is commonly practiced does not work.

Misguided efforts at discipline breed resentment and division. The person disciplined simply moves to another church, starts another church, creates a division in the present church, or may even abandon church altogether and continue in open rebellion. In such situations pastors may be tempted to become the wrong kind of peacemakers—ones that accept peace at any price. In none of these cases do either repentance or restoration take place.

This absence of repentance in corrective church discipline should concern us greatly. Obviously there is sin in the church needing confession and forgiveness. Obviously Scripture leads us to believe corrective discipline will work at least some of the time. For example, when Jesus says, ". . . if he [the sinning brother] listens to you, . . ." the expression implies much more than a physical hearing. It implies a heeding and a repenting.

Grassroots Discipline

If our efforts at corrective discipline are biblical and yet never produce repentance at least in some offenders, then we must be going about it in the wrong way. The commonest error is to suppose that authority figures administer discipline best. Awe of them will bring repentance and love of them good behavior. However, parents and school teachers are painfully aware that habits and characters are powerfully shaped by peer pressure. It is the censure of the community that brings repentance, and the plaudits of the community that stimulate exemplary behavior.

Roland Allen makes wise comments on the necessity of grassroots discipline and the impotence of authoritarianism from the perspective of a missionary. He describes the problems with discipline-from-above in the Anglican community in China at the beginning of this century:

> If a serious offence is committed, the foreign priest in charge of the district with or without the assistance of the local committee, inquires into the case; he reports to the bishop. The bishop either hears the case or accepts the report, excommunicates, and issues a sentence which is published in the church. But the church in which the offender lives feels little or no responsibility, and the man is not excommunicated by the majority. Consequently, the act has little effect. It does not come home to the offender; it does not come home to the church. A man can afford to present a stubborn front to the fulminations of a foreigner, who is perhaps only an occasional visitor and is always a foreigner. He cannot so treat the excommunication of (by) his neighbours. . . . What he needs is the public censure of the majority of his fellow churchmen to awaken his conscience. If the majority of his fellow churchmen do not avoid him and cast him out, it is little use for a formal sentence of exclusion to be issued. . . . That does no good; it very often only does harm. It hardens the man without humbling or instructing him.[1]

Inappropriate discipline hardens sinners. Not only does it fail to restore. It reinforces wrong attitudes and petrifies distorted character. John Owen, a major Puritan theologian, who could never be accused of minimizing the authority of church leaders, comments, "It cannot be denied that the interest, yea, the power of the whole church, in the fraternity of it, is to be greatly considered herein; for indeed whenever the apostle treats of it [church discipline] he doth not any where recommend it unto the officers of the church . . . but unto the whole church or the brethren therein. . . . They are obliged in point of spiritual interest, as they care for their own souls, to concur in the rejection of the offender."[2] Discipline by the community is not only biblical. It *restores* sinners.

Jack's Story

Does corrective church discipline work in practice? Of course it does. While we should do things because they are right (because Scripture teaches them) and not because they work, the fact is that church discipline as Ken and I have described it and practiced it does work. It does bring brothers and sisters back to God (restoration) and back into fellowship (reconciliation) and back to freedom in Christ. It also enhances the vitality of Christian communities where it is valued and practiced. Quantitative growth can also result. C. Peter Wagner has commented that there is a positive correlation between corrective church discipline and church growth, especially in Third World countries. Even in the West the practice of such discipline is associated with growing churches.

Certainly some churches botch corrective church discipline catastrophically. For example, it is sometimes used as a political weapon and as a means of venting personal hostility or bitterness. Yet when churches follow both the letter and the spirit of Christ's instructions, they see the fruits he promised.

I made careful and detailed notes in recording the story of a clean-cut, manly-looking, unmarried government employee in his early thirties. We will call him Jack.

At the time of the interview several months had passed since Jack had been restored to a godly walk. He had been dismissed from his fellowship for drug abuse and ongoing promiscuity which had failed to respond to firm, but kindly counseling over a period of time. He belongs to a church that takes discipline seriously. Most church members are converts from non-Christian backgrounds. Curiously, but as is frequently the case, Jack's teaching ministry continued to be used by God even while Jack persisted in sin.

He had an open, friendly face and looked me in the eye as I asked him how he felt about the whole affair. Jack replied, "I thank the Lord for this means [of correction] that God has given us. . . . I was able finally to see what I could do, and it led me to fear all I could be."

How did he feel about the elders? "I never did love them until after I was disciplined. I had this love-hate thing with them. See, they were my friends too. I could really accuse them. I had them half believing me. I had set up this sophisticated system of defense. I had had feelings of great sorrow, but nothing in my heart had changed."

How had they handled him in the end? "They said, 'You have proven to us by your actions that our words can do nothing for you.' I couldn't deny they had made the effort to help me. There was no way I could say that. This made the excommunication really effective. I *knew* they'd done everything they could. Yet it didn't have to be that way. I could have repented long before. I knew that."

How did it feel to be told he had to leave? "I thought, 'God! What . . . ?' I got into this defeatist attitude."

And when they came to see him to accept him back some weeks later? "I had to tell them, 'I don't know if I've really changed.' " But had he? His eyes shone, "I've learned so much. It was incredible! All these new things about God . . ." At that point his eyes filled with tears of joy.

Was the tendency to sin gone then? "No. No, it's still there." He paused. "If I find my thoughts beginning to go that way again I go back and read the whole thing again [a careful account he had kept of the period, including his thoughts and evaluations of what was going on] to get my thinking straight."

I was deeply moved, as I have been on several occasions, both by the joy and the indescribable purity of the atmosphere where

I have found myself talking with a Christian who has come through such an experience. He was restored. That is to say, his heart was tender toward God and the things of God. And from the reports of others I learned of a new stability in his character and a consistency in his walk.

Let us look at the key principles that Jack's story raises. First, Jack's heart had grown harder and his skill in deceiving himself and his friends became more finely honed before he was excommunicated. The dishonesty sin breeds is infinitely more destructive and difficult to deal with than the initial sin itself, be that sin greed, drunkenness, promiscuity or whatever. Indeed the real battle is the battle for honesty and openness of heart.

Second, Jack had a genuine heart for God even while he continued to play with sin. One might argue that he could not have been sincere in his hunger for God during this time. But in arguing this way we forget that it is God who in his faithfulness and by his Holy Spirit implants longings for himself in our hearts so that our desire for him can remain. The point is that the longing can never be satisfied while we continue in sin.

Next, Jack took initiative in looking for ways to serve God. Apparently the Holy Spirit used his service even while he continued to sin. Here we face one of the mysteries of God's ways, his right to give spiritual gifts and use them through whomever he will (Mt 7:21-23). He can use his enemies as easily as his friends. Stones could cry out his praises. But of course Jack's longing for fellowship with God went unsatisfied, even though God apparently blessed his ministry. For it is not being used that counts, but having fellowship with the Lord of glory. This is life's greatest reward.

Lastly, the church leaders' loving ministry in warning Jack contributed greatly to the effectiveness of the discipline. I not only talked at length with the leadership, but sat in and observed them as they carried out their disciplinary procedures. Although they had not verbalized the reconciliation principle, it was clear that their attitude fostered reconciliation, and therefore facilitated restoration. The fact that they followed up on Jack even after he was excommunicated bears witness to this.

Restoration and Conformity

Was Jack's restoration (return to godly behavior) secured by social pressure? Should Scripture and the Holy Spirit's conviction be the only sources of true repentance? Conformity concerns outward behavior. It does not necessarily spring from a changed attitude of heart. By and large it is the enemy of the church. Conformity (or *conformism,* the tendency to behave like the majority around) can be a sign of immaturity and carnality. Inside church buildings and at weeknight church meetings, we Christians tend to adopt the mannerisms, the dress, the speech and the behavioral patterns that prevail at such places and times. Our conformity may be an outward aping without any inward change.

But social pressure to conform need not always be wrong if the goal is to bring one back to righteousness in a loving manner. Jack's heart had changed. The fellowship's authority and social pressure had played a part in his restoration. But the pressure was a divinely appointed means by which the Holy Spirit was able to get at Jack's heart. His heart was not changed by *mere* enforcement of rules, but by the God who used that enforcement as his instrument.

Of course there are dangers. One danger Roland Allen saw was that of authoritarianism, a danger common among some Christians, both charismatic and traditional, which we discussed in chapter three. Terms like *covering* and *umbrella* are often used in teaching a form of authoritarianism which has the appearance of godliness, but which is not biblical and which fosters infantilism rather than freedom and growth among church members.

But does any form of church discipline avert this danger and lead to restoration *and* freedom? How can any form of coercion, even "voluntary coercion" do so? The seeds of the answer lie in all that we have been discussing up to this point. We discuss them more fully in the next chapter.

7

Discipline
That
Sets Free

FREEDOM IS A LAME MAN WALKING, leaping and praising God.

Freedom is a woman with chronic obstructive lung disease able to breathe easily.

Picture a woman in a hospital bed. She is overweight and has just finished sneaking a cigarette. She sucks air into herself by an immense effort, neck muscles tightening with each breath. Her lips are blue. Her eyes stare in fear at the walls of her room. If Jesus were to touch her, or if some miracle injection could give her new lungs, you might (is your imagination vivid enough?) see the fear give place to surprise, then delight. The fight to capture air would be over. Her lips would turn pink. She would get out of the bed and run down the corridor shouting, "I can breathe! I can breathe!" For her that would be freedom.

Freedom is a blind man stepping into light, a deaf girl released from a world of silence, a terrorized victim of political oppression discovering he can express his real opinions to anybody any-where, and can walk out of his front door without checking to see whether the secret police are around.

By Design

One might think that corrective church discipline would bring an atmosphere of repressive fear in the church. But healthy discipline should have the opposite result. To be free first means not being what you once were—bound, limited, fearful. Then it means taking a quantum leap closer to what God meant all human beings to be.

Freedom is not "doing what you want." That idea is absurd. We think we know what we want, but we don't. We only know urges and hungers, the pull of illusions. A drug addict "wants" a fix. His "want" is slavery. A murderer "wants" to kill. He is both victim and victimizer. Drug addicts and murderers may be accountable for their actions but, paradoxically, they are far from being free. Do what you like and you will discover you are the slave and the victim of what you hate.

No, freedom is doing what you were designed to do, doing it with power and joy. As a creature formed by God you were designed to serve, love, enjoy and glorify God eternally. In being what you are designed to be you will find joy and freedom.

We yearn for freedom. Christians and non-Christians crave it alike. But some of us give up and pathetically accept a dreary life of semienslavement. Yet the dream persists. One reason for the Me Generation of the seventies and for the current fad for discovering our full human potential arises from suppressed yearnings for freedom. Human potentialists offer us a self-esteem, self-worth, self-development of the humanist, man-centered vari-ety. We mistake what they offer for freedom.

Our hunger explains the unbelievable growth and influence of the human potential movement, a loosely knit movement of theorists who offer us what we think we long for. Its teachings and gimmickry have spilled into a literary cataract of semipsycholog-ical Christian books from which a thirsty Christian public drinks in vain.

But freedom is not found in the pursuit of self-fulfillment, self-esteem or self-gratification. All of these ultimately ensnare. Freedom needs a context in the way a football player needs a playing field. The players do not gain freedom by running with the ball outside the bounds of the field. Our freedom arises within the context of a God-created universe.

Sin enslaves (Jn 8:34). Jesus frees (Jn 8:36). He frees us because he is the truth, the truth that bursts through the darkness of our shuttered intellects to bring light beyond our intellects into our very hearts (Jn 8:32). Freedom, like reconciliation, lies at the heart of the gospel. Jesus died that we might be set free. As Christians we "once lived in the passions of our flesh, following the desires of body and mind" (Eph 2:3). God had given us up to impurity (Rom 1:24), to dishonorable passions (Rom 1:26) and to a "base mind," a mind controlled by "wants" rather than by truth (Rom 1:28-32). The purpose of our redemption and our justification was that we might no longer be slaves (Gal 4:7-8). When the Son made us free, we were to be "free indeed" (Jn 8:36).

So far we have been talking about freedom only in personal terms, as though it were an individual matter. But we saw earlier that the results of sin were widespread, involving the relationship between men and women as well as between each and God. If sin-caused alienation is multidirectional, so is sin-caused enslavement. Sin enslaves society as well as individuals.

Cain's "freedom" to express his rage cost Abel his life. Oppression, enslavement and exploitation of human beings by other human beings took root in primitive society and flourishes today like a jungle, suffocating human freedoms. Even in the West, where we should be extremely grateful for the freedom we enjoy, social freedom is relative. The president of the United States, for example, is a prisoner of his office. He may not take an unplanned, spontaneous stroll even around the White House grounds. Political and financial power bring enslavements of their own. Sin destroyed the possibility of true social freedom.

Social freedom springs from the loving responsibility of a society's members toward one another. And this in turn springs from their having discovered that God is a God of grace who longs to pardon sinners. The more people perceive the glory of a gracious God, the more willing they are to be open, to repent, to trust him. The more they do so, the more they love one another. And the more people love and care for one another, the fewer laws they need to govern them and the smaller the police force needs to be to make those laws stick.

You can smell social freedom. I remember crossing the Yugoslav border into Austria a few years after World War 2 on the pillion of a motorbike. A friend and I had been contacting a needy church and supplying them with clothing (the bike was large and powerful) and Scripture portions. We had been introduced both to the normal and the underground aspects of the church's activities and had undergone intensive interrogation by the authorities who wanted to track down the destination of the clothing and literature. (They failed.)

We crossed the border into Austria at night. After a few miles I became aware of a sense of exhilaration and joy. To be more precise, I *felt* the exhilaration of freedom, but wondered whether I was experiencing a psychological release following days of tension. However, I noticed a small difference once the border was crossed. In the Austrian villages through which we passed, people were sitting round lighted tables in open-air cafés.

"Notice anything?" my friend asked.

"Freedom?" I countered.

"So you felt it too. I wondered if it was just me."

It was the little things that cued us to the freedom in Austria. So it is the little things in church life that will cue us to an atmosphere of freedom. Are certain topics taboo? Are certain expressions of concern or affection or joy looked down on? These indicate a lack of freedom. Our actions and attitudes are restricted, inhibited.

If what we are saying is true, then churches where Christian love and responsibility abound (they do not abound in all churches) should be churches where social freedom is both present and felt. "Where the Spirit of the Lord is, there is freedom," Paul tells us (2 Cor 3:17). If then we ask the question, "Does church discipline produce an atmosphere of freedom in the church?" we might begin by inquiring whether church discipline is compatible with the presence of the Holy Spirit.

Where the Spirit Is

Freedom is one of the four goals of church discipline. Christ paid a high price for our liberty, and we enjoy it all too little. How does church discipline free us as individuals and as local churches?

Paul's words in 2 Corinthians 3:17 may help us to understand how the gospel frees, frees us both individually and corporately. For of course it is the Holy Spirit who frees us by revealing the gospel to us. And whereas many of the verses we quoted earlier about freedom referred to individual freedom, the Corinthian passage (2 Cor 3:12-18) deals both with corporate and individual freedom.

Liberty abounds in the presence of the Spirit. Truth is the means whereby he imparts freedom. The Spirit sets us free by snatching from our eyes the veil that hides truth. He sets us free as individuals: "When a man turns to the Lord the veil is removed" (2 Cor 3:16). However, Paul's emphasis really rests on the freedom of populations. The Israelites as a race had hardened hearts because of the veil that hid the truth from them. As a people we are freed as the Spirit reveals God's face to us and changes us into his image.

The gospel, the truth, sets us free, but is church discipline another means the Spirit may use? We firmly believe that only church discipline which is an extension of and part of the gospel itself is true discipline. Therefore, freedom *must* be an aim in church discipline. For freedom Christ died and rose. Church discipline must aim at training church members in the practicalities of the gospel. It must enlighten. It must remove veils from eyes. It must reconcile, restore, purify. It must enable members to trust one another more completely. And in so doing it will liberate. One person who had been disciplined told us, "I never saw it before. I never saw how sick and deceitful my own heart was, nor how good God was. I never saw that God had taken my heart of stone away . . ."

You may not have run across them, but churches really exist

where discipline creates freedom. Their leaders have found the secret of helping their members to avoid sin without putting them in shackles. The liberation arises from increased spiritual enlightenment, and from a growth of mutual trust. Yet tragically most forms of discipline fail both to suppress sin and to create freedom. We have said before that wrongly exercised discipline drives people deeper into darkness. But right discipline leads them into light. It is a weapon Christ gave to his church, and there are greater dangers in neglecting it than in restoring it. There is good reason to fear it, just as there is good reason to fear carving knives, electricity and fire. But we still carve roasts, turn on switches and enjoy warmth. In malicious hands a surgeon's scalpel can kill. But its very sharpness contains an equal potential for healing.

So it is with church discipline. Its potential for destruction is matched by its potential not only for peace among brothers and sisters, restoration of sinners and the sanctification of churches, but for spiritual liberty as well.

A Shining Cockroach

It is easy to see how discipline and training can liberate individuals. The free and airy grace of ballerinas, the technical fluency of instrumentalists, the gravity-defying leap of the high jumper all are examples of the effects of discipline and training. But the "freedom you can smell" is something we also need in churches. We began to understand it when we saw that a free society is one where the members love one another, trust one another and take responsibility for one another. But we can also approach the problem by looking into the nature and causes of the opposite of freedom—legalism or bondage.

We become legalists whenever we try to keep our consciences clear by keeping a set of rules. Rules are important. They are meant to be observed. But they are not the means by which our consciences are kept clean. Christian consciences are cleansed by the blood of Christ (Heb 9:14). Legalism arises when, perhaps without realizing what we are doing, we assume that a clean conscience arises from the sacrifice of Christ *plus our postconver-*

sion performance in keeping Christian rules. In this way a veil of darkness has fallen on our faces, making us slaves to our evil consciences. Thus legalism is never corrective church discipline. For legalism pulls us away from following Christ toward another gospel, another gospel that says the cross is not enough. True church discipline, however, calls us to follow Christ alone and receive his freedom.

Legalists may struggle constantly against a sense of guilt, or they may be sublimely free of guilt-feelings. But in both cases their feelings, whether of guilt or of freedom from guilt are related to rule-keeping. Guilt-ridden people struggle but are aware of their failures. Guilt-free legalists are Christians who, like the Pharisees, bend the rules to fit their actual behavior, or who concentrate on the rules they do keep and ignore the rest. In their case the Spirit needs to teach them, perhaps through corrective church discipline, the exceeding deceitfulness of their hearts.

Legalism is clearly a sin against the God of grace and mercy. Yet we are rarely thinking about God at all when we begin to behave like legalists. We are usually thinking about our fellow human beings, our neighbors, our workmates, our families and our fellow believers. They determine our behavior far more than we are aware.

Paul Tournier writes about the *persona,* the mask worn by Greek actors to indicate their roles in ancient dramas. He points out that on the stage of life we too wear personas; that is, we assume different personality styles in different situations. We do so by habit. We wear one persona when parenting children, another when asking questions of a lecturer and yet another when being introduced to strangers. In itself there is nothing wrong with this. It makes sense to behave differently when we put our children to bed from the way we do when we give evidence in a court of law.

But there are more sinister reasons for wearing masks. Sometimes we do not want people to see our real faces. We have shames and guilts to hide. If some masks were torn from us, we would be exposed and naked. Our need for acceptance and approval keeps us clutching our false fronts fiercely. Thus we are enslaved to our legalistic facades. It is possible that even those who know us best have never seen all of our faces. We send out antennae like those of a cockroach, probing the atmosphere around us. Our antennae pick up even imaginary vibrations of disapproval and concentrate (have you ever observed a cockroach carefully?) on exterior polishing. Cockroaches actually *shine* in the light. In this respect they are not unlike some Christians who have a surface sheen only.

However unaware we are normally of our personas, we are uncomfortable when we approach God while wearing them. God sees through our masks and we know it. Our souls are naked in his presence. Therefore, we shrink from intimate contact with him, hardly knowing why, clinging to our shames and guilts and turning our faces away from him. We resist the freedom we could enjoy if we were to let him rid us of our heavy masks.

Legalism and Local Congregations

We are probably all legalists by nature, but certain types of preaching and certain administrators and leaders may worsen our natural tendency. We have already noted that some church leaders fail to understand the difference between spiritual and worldly authority. Occasionally, especially if they are young in age and inexperienced, they may say, "You must submit to me because God has placed me over you." Now while such words may be true, they are words that never fall from the lips of true leaders because the authority of true leaders springs from spiritual power. Such words prove the speaker's unfitness for his task. They too can enslave us to another gospel rather than draw us to the freedom of the cross.

As for legalism-producing preachers, they come in a variety of forms. Some are obnoxious, others merely mislead while yet others seem highly spiritual. Such preachers may delight their listeners by condemning the sins and errors of other groups, thus inducing a form of self-righteousness in themselves and in their hearers. Others may increase the load of legalism by engaging in aren't-we-all-awful preaching. They point to the congregation's general lack of dedication and admit their own lukewarmness. But instead of offering solutions, they merely lament the sad state of affairs and leave the general impression we ought to do better. We emerge from such sermons depressed.

Legalism alienates us from one another. It creates an atmosphere which inhibits true fellowship. It inhibits our freedom to share our personal weaknesses and ask for help, making some of us suspect we have weaknesses no one else shares or would understand.

We are surrounded by men and women who profess faith in Christ yet are victims of every sort of vice and sin. The sins are practiced mostly in secret. We are also surrounded by a world where these same sins increase daily. Converted sinners are going to need help and deliverance. But from us? In the condition we are?

The freedom they need must come from Christ. It will come when hearts (theirs and ours) have been deeply convicted of sin. It will come as we, then they, discover the sufficiency of Christ to shatter the chains of guilt, so that we rediscover overflowing joy and an astonishing reduction of a desire to sin. It will come when sinners find models in churches, churches where Christians both teach and model open, accepting, understanding relationships. We must become brothers and sisters who can level with them in love.

And when they fail, as we all will from time to time, freedom will come from that kind of church discipline which under God's Spirit renews our horror of sin and our sinfulness, while awakening us afresh to the astounding grace of God.

8

The
Matthew
Passage

WE HAVE TOUCHED ON MATTHEW 18:15-22 many times so far in this book. It is time to take a concentrated look at it (and 1 and 2 Corinthians in the next chapter) in a systematic fashion.

It cannot be a coincidence that the classical passage on corrective church discipline in the New Testament follows on the heels of the parable of the man who left his ninety-nine sheep to search for the one that was lost. The story sets the stage for what follows, reminding us again of the centrality of reconciliation. For what is the parable about? What is its thrust? Curiously the point is missed in the very title we have given it. We have misunderstood the sense in which Jesus is using the word *lost*.

As noted earlier, the word can be used in one of two ways. Commonly we concentrate (as we do in the three parables in Luke 15) on the plight of what or who had been lost. We rightly compare the sheep, the coin and the son with lost sinners. But *lost* can also carry the sense of lost *by* someone. For every item lost there is an *item-loser.* "I think I've lost my wallet," says Mary looking pale and distraught. Mary is understandably upset. "It's got over a hundred dollars in it plus my driver's license and all my credit cards. I'm sure it was in my purse when I left home . . ." When the wallet is found her delight and relief are commensurate with the distress she felt when it was missing. She ardently hugs Jim who discovered it beside some papers she had left on his desk.

The parable should be entitled, "The Searching Shepherd," for the focus is on the concern of the shepherd who has sustained the loss, rather than on the plight of the sheep. Luke 15:1-2 makes this very plain. The parables were told by Jesus to explain God's feelings about sinners and his reaction when they are restored to him.

Thus at the outset of the classical passage on discipline we are reminded that a sinning brother is a brother whose fellowship we have lost. Our approach to him is a quest to restore fellowship. Sin has brought alienation. Reconciliation is needed to overcome it.

To Judge or Not to Judge

"If your brother sins against you . . ." (Mt 18:15). *Brother,* of course, means brother or sister in Christ (though we will use *brother* for convenience in our discussion since that is the word used in the text). We have also discussed the expression *against you,* concluding that although the phrase is missing in some early manuscripts, the fact is unimportant. Other passages urge us to go whether the sin is directed against us or not.

The next question is a thorny one. Do we have the right to say that someone else has sinned? Or even to think it? Are we not warned against judging others? "Judge not, that you be not judged," Jesus commands in Matthew 7:1. "If we are not supposed to judge," we think to our relief, "then we don't have to talk to our fellow Christians about their sins." But Matthew 18:15 implies judgment. One can't approach a brother about sin without having made at least a preliminary judgment of some kind.

The meaning of the word *judge,* however, varies in different contexts. "Do not judge by appearances, but judge with right judgment," Jesus advises the Jews (Jn 7:24). The same word is used in Matthew 7:1. But in the first case we are being told, "Don't be critical of others. Don't look down on them and feel you are better than they. Don't play the magistrate." In the second case he is saying, "Be discerning. Don't jump to hasty conclusions. Be careful to judge justly."

Thus Jesus teaches us two things about judging others. First, we must be very cautious about our attitudes to others and must avoid condemnation. On the other hand, we are taught to exercise discernment about the sins of our brothers and sisters, but to be cautious about jumping to hasty conclusions. Clearly the second warning is important if the sin in question is against us. For we might be mistaken in thinking we have been wronged. We might have misunderstood a remark or been offended because we misconstrued an innocent action. This is one reason why private sins and wrongs should be kept private and not made public. It is also a reason for guarding ourselves against an unforgiving spirit.

Obviously it will be necessary for us to judge in the sense of assessing or weighing the actions of our fellow Christians from time to time. Not to do so will be another way of acting as though we were situational ethicists, contextualizing other people's sins. Murder is murder. Lies are lies. At times it is our duty to deal with them. And if we are helping to build up younger Christians, we shall need to assess their spiritual progress or lack of it in smaller matters. But before doing so we must be careful to arrive at sound and accurate conclusions.

The Subtle Snare of Gossip

"Go and tell him his fault, between you and him alone" (Mt 18:15). Go and tell him? That's rough. A thousand excuses and rationalizations for not going at once present themselves. "I could be mistaken." So why not find out and set your mind at rest? "I might offend him." What you really mean is that there might be unpleasantness, and he might get upset with you. If you really care about him you will be prepared to risk that possibility. But we will deal with the *how* of going in chapter ten.

"Perhaps he needs to see a counselor or a psychiatrist." Perhaps. But how will you find out unless you go and talk to him about what is bothering you? "I'm so inexperienced at these things." Too inexperienced to seek reconciliation with a brother? Or was reconciliation not what you had in mind? And in any case how will you gain experience if you fail him at this point? We gain experience only by doing.

No, the command is clear. "The reconciling approach is personal," asserts John Howard Yoder.[1] Our excuses about being judgmental are the feeble rationalizations of the scared. Jesus commands us to go.

"But perhaps I should ask someone's advice first?" No. That above all must be avoided. You are to tell him his fault "between you and him alone." The beauty of Christ's instructions is that they avoid gossip. It is best that in the first instance no one knows about the matter. Publicity might hinder reconciliation. Suppose when you eventually do go you discover you were mistaken? Already you might have done your brother the injustice of spreading a wrong impression about him, a wrong impression that might remain in the confused memory of the person whose advice you sought, even though you later tried to correct it. You might get a smile and an, "Oh, I'm so glad you were wrong!" But slander sticks in the memory more easily than correction of slander.

"But shouldn't I pray about it with someone? Wouldn't it be good if I had some prayer backing?" Prayer backing? Or just plain backing? Prayer can be a form of gossip. It can be a "spiritual" way of avoiding your duty to treat the matter with the utmost confidentiality. Any attempt not to keep the matter between you and your brother (or sister) alone is at once suspect. It is only too easy to deceive ourselves about our motives.

No. For the present the matter is to remain sealed. It is to concern you, your brother and God alone. No gossip, "spiritual" or otherwise.

What might happen if you should obey Christ and go, seeking reconciliation? What might the brother do? There are several possibilities. (1.) He might admit the wrong but insist that it's just his business. (2.) He might admit the wrong and ask your help with his problem, thus opening the door to reconciliation. (3.) He might admit the wrong and freely repent of it, in which case reconciliation would be accomplished. (4.) He might deny the wrong and satisfy you completely that you were mistaken, again bringing reconciliation about. (5.) He might lie in such a way that you know he is lying. (6.) He might deny the charge, and leave you with unresolved doubts in your mind. (7.) He might refuse to discuss it at all.

We shall consider these possibilities in part three. What matters for the moment is that several of the above possibilities constitute further arguments (if arguments are needed to back anything Christ clearly commands) for going personally, privately to the brother, without prior discussion with anybody. Once when I failed to do this the consequences were tragic.

But let us suppose that you find your suspicions are confirmed. He confesses that he has indeed been drinking to excess, that his job is in jeopardy and his marriage is beginning to crack. He has been miserable over the past year but, say, a week previously, he attended his first Alcoholics Anonymous meeting. Perhaps, he says, there is hope.

He pours out his misery, the appalling effects of the whole business on his relationship with God, his bewilderment that such a thing could happen to him (he had always been a disciplined person who seemed to have such control of his life) and the loneliness and alienation he has sensed toward his Christian friends. Once he gets going you can hardly stop him. He is overwhelmed with guilt, but amazed that God still loves and can forgive him. He is more grateful than he can tell you that he now has a chance to talk to someone, to someone who (hopefully) does not immediately reject him. So where do you go from there?

You have gained your brother. He has listened to you. That which alienated you no longer does. Christ's main concern has been satisfied. But what do you do next (apart from rejoicing and praying with him)? Well, perhaps nothing. A lot depends on your brother's needs at that point. But if you are asking, "Do I have the authority to pronounce him clean?" our answer in this case would be yes. "Who can forgive sins but God alone?" you may ask (along with the scribes and the Pharisees). True, the prerogative is his alone. But he calls on us to declare forgiveness to one another and to assure one another of it. Or have we in our post-Reformation fear of excessive sacerdotalism forgotten the doctrine of the priesthood of *all* believers?

In any case what alternatives do you have? Biblically your next step is clearly not that of confronting him with two or three witnesses, and certainly not of telling the whole church. You long, perhaps, for some more authoritative support. The responsibility is heavy. But that is your problem, not your friend's. You would like to take him to your pastor? But does he wish to go? Would your motive be to let the responsibility rest on someone else's shoulders, whatever your friend's real needs might be? What will he gain by seeing someone else? If Christ has pardoned him and he feels no immediate need of further help, the most valuable aid you may be able to render is that of your personal and prayerful fellowship as he gets on his feet again.

Unless church members are able to minister to one another in this way, we shall be confronted with an impossible situation once God's Spirit begins to work among us. For sin is so common and so serious in Christian circles that church officers will be overwhelmed by its sheer volume if they alone are called on to deal with it.

The Witnesses

"But if he does not listen, take one or two others along with you, that every word may be confirmed by the evidence of two or three witnesses" (Mt 18:16). The sentence has its roots in the law of Moses. But we must be careful to keep our goals clearly in mind. Witnesses may become necessary to protect the accused as well as to confirm the accuser. But its goal is never to condemn. We do not drag others into the matter to nail an opponent to the wall. Nor do we bring in witnesses until we have done all we can ourselves to effect a reconciliation. What gain is there in witnesses?

There is the gain of added solemnity. The original matter does not become more serious, but both the offended brother and the offending brother inevitably begin to take it more seriously. We also gain added wisdom. There may be a perspective which neither has thought about, for the witnesses may benefit both the offender and the offended. They witness not just the response of the accused but also the words of the accuser. If the issue becomes public, both parties have witnesses of what was and was not said. They may also add objectivity, becoming parties to a reconciliation where both are at fault or throw light on matters which otherwise remained obscure.

And let us suppose for a moment that the offender has indeed offended and now repents, or even asks for help. It may be that practical measures are called for (of a nature to be discussed later), practical measures that the group may talk over with the offender and implement for his well-being.

Whom should we choose for witnesses? Some people would opt for church elders or deacons though the New Testament nowhere specifies this. Certainly there is value in choosing older and more experienced people. On the other hand, a younger person, one more in tune with the setting surrounding a younger person's sin, may also prove helpful. To some extent the nature of the problem may determine who is involved. In one case where Ken was consulted, only one person extra was needed.

A single girl fresh from Bible school was advised by an older single woman in the church to try having an affair. The older woman, who was active in a children's work in the church, claimed to speak from experience. Indeed she was currently involved, or so she said, with one of the church deacons whose marriage was in difficulties. She was "helping him" by providing the kind of solace the marriage was not providing.

She knew that the woman's advice and purported conduct was wrong but had found it hard to answer her from Scripture. The younger girl, nervous and very hesitant, approached the deacon. The deacon looked her in the eye and said, "We'd better go together and talk to her about it, hadn't we?"

Confronted with both of them, the older woman admitted that while her life had not been free from past affairs (a fact the deacon knew), she was not then having and had not ever had an affair with him. When he asked her about the alleged difficulties in his marriage, she faltered. Well . . . once when she had called him by telephone she had heard his wife shouting.

She asserted, nevertheless, that there was nothing wrong in having affairs, and clung to her right to have them. The deacon asked whether they both might spend time with her going over the Scriptures which dealt with such matters. She replied, "Does that mean I can't have the children any more?" and was told that their first concern was that she herself should understand what sin was all about. The three of them set two or three dates to meet, to read the relevant Scriptures and pray over them.

I do not know how the matter ended, but the incident illustrates a number of points. The courage of the younger woman in approaching the deacon paid off. There was no juicy gossip circulating round the church about an imaginary affair between a deacon and a Sunday-school teacher. The deacon's own no-nonsense approach was also helpful here.

There were additional spin-offs. Neither the younger woman nor the deacon had entertained high opinions of each other previously, largely because they knew each other only superficially. A mutual respect arose between them. And in the disciplinary process not only the older woman, but also the young woman was able to learn from Scripture passages dealing with sexuality.

It is worth noting that the deacon saw it to be his duty to spend time with both of them in the Scriptures before bringing the matter before the whole church, an action which perhaps never became necessary.

A Gentile and a Tax Collector

"If he refuses to listen to them, tell it to the church; and if he refuses to listen even to the church, let him be to you as a Gentile and a tax collector" (Mt 18:17). If you want to kill gossip, there is no better weapon for doing so than a clear public statement of the truth. Gossip thrives on rumor and half-truths. We may seem to be belaboring the theme of gossip, but we make no apology for doing so. Gossip is a sign of the absence of proper church discipline. It is also a great evil, itself calling for corrective church discipline. Nothing so poisons fellowship as gossip. But let us look more carefully at the verse quoted above.

The group of witnesses has failed in its attempt. Reconciliation has not come about. One last attempt is to be made. The matter is to be brought before the whole church, so that the offender and the church alike will be brought face to face with the awfulness of sin and the supreme value God places on holiness and on reconciliation. For it is not the character of the specific sin that matters, but the principle of sin, the deliberate hardening of a heart in rebellion, the rebellion that called for the Incarnation of the Son of God and the sacrifice of the Son of man.

What value does the procedure have? Are there dangers and abuses we should beware of? What role should church leadership play in this solemn procedure? In an earlier chapter we quoted some wise words from Roland Allen, who in a missionary setting made the clear distinction between the whole church and the leaders of the church. His remarks bear repetition. Where a missionary or a pastor acts on behalf of the church, Allen points out, "the church in which the offender lives feels little or no responsibility and the man is not excommunicated by the majority. Consequently the act has little effect. It does not come home to the offender; it does not come home to the church. A man can afford to present a stubborn front to the fulminations of a [church leader]. He cannot so treat excommunication of his neighbours. . . . What he needs is the public censure of the majority of his fellow churchmen."[2]

We hope it is clear by now that such solemn measures are only called for *when every other attempt to bring about repentance, restoration and reconciliation has been thoroughly explored and has failed.* It is here that the abuses come in.

In some churches in Manitoba, Canada, young couples who have engaged in sexual relations before marriage are required to stand before the congregation and confess their sin, before the church will proceed with their marriage or accept them back into fellowship. However well-intentioned this procedure is, it has no biblical warrant and is contrary to the whole spirit of church discipline. It is to be deplored, and should be done away with. Suppose that only those immediately concerned with the wrong are aware of what had happened. Suppose that true repentance has already taken place. In that case the procedure spreads unnecessary shame and embarrassment, and contributes to self-righteous gossip.

Usually, the idea behind this kind of system is that the couple have wronged the church by their sin and must apologize. But this idea is nowhere found in Scripture. The confession merely panders to the congregation's sense of its own righteousness, and thus brings no cleansing in the church. You cannot foster self-righteousness and cleanse the congregation from sin at the same time. Church cleansing is needed where church members already know about what has happened and have adopted "broad-minded, loving" attitudes; self-righteous, judgmental attitudes; uncaring or indifferent attitudes; or have avoided responsibility by criticizing leadership and gossiping. Sin has spread as these attitudes have developed. Church members themselves need to be brought to repentance if the church is to be cleansed. But if the church knows nothing in the first place, the public confession merely opens the way to these same sinful attitudes.

And this, surely, is where church leadership comes in. They are responsible not primarily for the offending brother or sister but for the congregation as a whole. There can be no greater test of pastoral gifts than for the leaders to direct matters in such a way that the church is awakened to righteousness, to godly grief and to repentance, while at the same time the sinner is given a further opportunity to repent. We will explore this further in chapter ten.

And if the sinner remains obdurate? Then the true state of affairs must be recognized by all. Alienation, true spiritual alienation, is actually present. It already has divided brother from brother, sister from sister. Therefore, what has already taken place must be recognized openly for what it is. Earth must confirm what heaven has already seen and judged. The brother must be to the church "as a Gentile and a tax collector."

Later, as we look at the Corinthian passage, we must ask how this is carried out in practice. For the present we must ask what it means. Righteous Jews hated and despised Gentiles and tax collectors. They shunned Gentiles because they feared being defiled, and tax collectors because they were traitors who collaborated with the Romans and who lined their own pockets. Was Jesus calling for similar attitudes toward unrepentant offenders? His words are often taken to reflect this spirit. But is it what he really meant?

The break in social contact might need to be as complete, but the spirit of the Jews toward tax collectors is alien to all we have been describing. Christ died for the ungodly. The heart of God still reaches out to rebels and sinners, to those who are under discipline, no less than those who have never known reconciliation. And it was indeed just such people who were responding to Jesus' message of reconciliation. We must be careful then that the words *tax collector* and *Gentile* do not cause us to adopt those judgmental and superior attitudes Christ so clearly warns us about. Rather, we are to mourn over tragedy in the body of Christ. We must still leave the door to forgiveness wide open, seeking to win, as Jesus did, those who have been cut off from fellowship by their sin.

The Authority of the Keys
The powers of the kingdom are about us. They are committed to us and we largely ignore them. The church suffers in consequence from a debilitating spiritual anemia.

Commenting on Matthew 18:15-20, Yoder writes, "The position suggested here seems to gather together the dangers of several ecclesiastical scarecrows: it gives more authority to the church than does Rome, trusts more to the Holy Spirit than does Pentecostalism, has more respect for the individual than humanism, makes moral demands more binding than puritanism, is more open to the given situation than the 'new morality.' If practiced it would change the life of churches more fundamentally than has yet been suggested by the currently popular discussions of changing church structures."[3]

Clearly, as some commentators suggest, whatever corrective discipline we carry out on earth, if it is conducted under the direction of the Holy Spirit and in accordance with Scripture, it will *have already been ratified in heaven*. Such is the meaning of the tenses in Matthew 18:18 according to some scholars. And this makes sense. For as we mentioned above, the final step of corrective discipline merely recognizes an alienation which is already present, and presumably recognized by heaven so to be.

"Truly, I say to you, whatever you bind on earth shall be bound in heaven, and whatever you loose on earth shall be loosed in heaven" (Mt 18:18). *Loose? Bind?* What do the words mean? Jesus has a specific meaning in mind. *To bind* means to withhold fellowship, to recognize formally the state of alienation which has come about. *To loose* means to forgive, to open one's arms wide to someone who is being reconciled.

To bind can also mean to forbid, to declare that certain actions are prohibited. *To loose* thus also means to permit, to declare that other actions are acceptable. These were the technical meanings of the words in Christ's day, and this was the way the doctors of the law commonly used them. The rulings on right and wrong as decided by the rabbis were encoded in the *halakah,* the "traditions of the elders," so that Jesus is handing on to the disciples powers reserved in Judah for recognized religious authorities.[4]

Does the church have such powers today? Ought local congregations to legislate what constitutes Christian behavior and what doesn't? To do so has led in the past to unnecessary strictures in some cases, permission to sin in others and a legalistic codification of behavior that focuses on outward acts to the neglect of a concern with motives. On the other hand, failure to do so can constitute failure to offer needed guidance and help. There are times when the church ought to take a stand on some form of behavior, even if it should be behavior not specifically condemned in Scripture.

When gin was the curse of the poor in London, the Salvation Army rightly insisted on abstinence for those who, when won for Christ, wanted to become members. It made no sense to expose new Christians to fierce temptation. Under those circumstances drinking exposed former drunks to ongoing alcoholism, penury and broken homes. And it made still less sense to have a double standard permitting mature Christians to drink while prohibiting younger Christians from doing so.

The danger of the *halakah* lay not only in its concern with externals, but with the rigid authoritarianism of tradition, an authoritarianism which Jesus challenged vigorously and persistently. We conclude then that congregations may at times have the duty to legislate behavior, but that they must be sensitive to the Holy Spirit both in regard to biblical principles and to changing social climates. They must be careful to avoid developing pseudo-Christian *halakahs* since there is enough of a focus on externals already. The question is a tricky one, but it cannot and should not be evaded.

In the Presence of Supreme Authority

"Again I say to you, if two of you agree on earth about anything they ask, it will be done for them by my Father in heaven. For where two or three are gathered in my name, there am I in the midst of them" (Mt 18:19-20). Beautiful words. A beautiful promise. Yet so often their context is forgotten. Jesus is still explaining about binding and loosing, about forgiving and rejecting from fellowship. He is reinforcing the idea that his people are given the terrible responsibility to remove from their fellowship someone who willfully and persistently refuses to repent, and also the authority to forgive and to receive sinners back when they turn from their sin and acknowledge their wrong.

He is making it doubly clear that heaven is behind them. Even if only two or three of them are involved in the painful (or the joyful) procedure, God's ear is open to them and heaven will back them. For is not the Lord Jesus present in their midst? At such moments they surround the throne at the right hand of the Majesty on high.

It is comforting to forget the context of the verses, and it may be legitimate to do so at times. But the words have to do primarily with corrective church discipline. The solemnity of the matter goes far beyond the gathering of a local congregation. It involves the powers of heaven, a fact which should solemnize all of us who take part in it and cause us both to tremble and yet to act decisively, knowing the One whose authority stands behind us and whose very presence is with us.

The Mystery of Four Hundred and Ninety

"Then Peter came up and said to him, 'Lord, how often shall my brother sin against me, and I forgive him? As many as seven times?' Jesus said to him, 'I do not say to you seven times, but seventy times seven' " (Mt 18:21-22). Literalists, numerologists and legalists can do what they like with the calculation. (Some authorities tell us the number is not four hundred and ninety times but seventy-seven.) The obvious meaning to the words of Jesus is that, as we have already seen, there is to be no limit to the number of times we forgive repentant sinners.

The point is also practical. Certain sins, particularly the socially unacceptable ones, are besetting sins. Habits have been formed that are hard to break. Christians who have been alcoholics fall off the wagon from time to time. Homosexuals who have been restored tend to fall back into temptation and sin. Gambling fever which proves easy to throw off in moments of joy, release and forgiveness returns to haunt those who have been gripped by it in the past. We wish it were not that way, but it is. Christ does not give us immunity to temptation, even though we cannot excuse ourselves when we fall back into sin.

After all, are not the most respectable among us subject to our private weaknesses, our angers, our bitternesses, our covetousness? Is it not true that we too have known release from sins and attitudes that return to haunt us in times when our faith seems at a low ebb? Should it surprise us then that our brothers and sisters should experience the same difficulty? Or that they might need to repent and to be received back again and again and again?

Our tendency is to say about someone else's sin, "Once a drunkard, always a drunkard." "She'll never stop her shoplifting. She doesn't really repent. She's just going through the motions to get back in." Hence the seventy times seven. We forgive. We go on forgiving. We never cease to forgive. By all means let us interview repentant sinners, but let us beware of becoming cynics, suspicious, judgmental. For our attitudes will boomerang on our own relationship with God. In being unwilling to forgive, unable to perceive true repentance in others because the sin has so often been repeated, we open ourselves to the Accuser of the brethren and begin to loose our own appreciation of God's forgiveness toward us. We become not only cynics, but guilt-ridden cynics. An old Puritan writer once said, "He who fails to forgive, destroys the bridge across which God's forgiveness comes to him."

Corrective church discipline begins with the recognition that sin produces alienation. It devotes itself to overcoming that alienation. But if it fails in its objective, the church, like the father in the story of the prodigal son, never ceases to long for and to wait for the return of the prodigal. And when the prodigal returns its delight knows no bounds.

9

The Corinthian Passages

A SCANDAL HAS TAKEN PLACE in the Corinthian church. Everyone knows that a member is sleeping with his father's wife. He is breaking Corinthian taboos, Jewish law and Roman custom. Yet the flagrant nature of the offense bothers Paul less than the church's attitude. "And you are arrogant! Ought you not rather to mourn? Let him who has done this be removed from among you" (1 Cor 5:2).

Mourn? Churches mourn at funerals. We don't mourn over scandals. We enjoy them. True, we indulge in sanctimonious gab-sessions over them. We say, "How shocking! What are things coming to?" And we shake our heads believing we are righteously deploring evil. But we fool ourselves. Mourning over sin is no longer de rigueur in Christian circles. Mourning is out. Rejoicing is in. Yet both have their place in the life of God's people.

Mourn for what? Mourn for an impure church! Mourn because

the church has sinned. She has broken her fellowship with a righteous God. She has grown lethargic, arrogant. She is too selfish to care about the sin of the fallen, too blind to see her own corruption. She needs eye salve to make her see. She needs repentance and true comfort. "Blessed are those who mourn, for they shall be comforted," said Jesus (Mt 5:4).

Paul has found out, perhaps through a letter from Chloe, that the Corinthian Christians are proud of their broad-mindedness (1 Cor 5:6). We pointed out in chapter five that things like arrogance and broad-mindedness spread the "leaven of malice and evil." The scandal has become public property, and when this is so a number of damaging attitudes develop. It matters little whether church members pride themselves on their tolerance, adopt critical and judgmental attitudes, or remain indifferent. Each of these attitudes is sinful. Each may pander to pride, to a lack of love, to gossip and even to divisiveness. But certainly not to a spirit of mourning.

Destroyed Flesh

Paul loses no time in telling them what to do. He himself has already pronounced judgment. "For though absent in body I am present in spirit, and as if present, I have already pronounced judgment in the name of the Lord Jesus on the man who has done such a thing. When you are assembled, and my spirit is present, with the power of our Lord Jesus, you are to deliver this man to Satan for the destruction of the flesh, that his spirit may be saved in the day of the Lord Jesus" (1 Cor 5:3-5). Leon Morris says, "He who was absent, and might have pleaded distance as an excuse for inaction, was not to be deterred from taking strong measures."[1] Paul is acting as their spiritual leader. His intervention is crucial, yet it does not serve as a substitute for the action they themselves must take. It is the church, not Paul, that must deliver the offender to Satan.

And it is the church that must do so _in the name_ and _with the power of the Lord Jesus._ This is what the complex Greek sentence seems to suggest. Some translations relate the expression _in the name of_ to Paul's own declaration of judgment. But certainly the words *with the power of* refer to the presence of Jesus among the Corinthians as they meet to act. Paul will be present in spirit (in no mystical sense, but in his thoughts and prayers), but the Lord Jesus will be present in power (Mt 18:20).

How do you deliver someone to Satan? No fate could be more horrifying. What terrible powers have been committed to us?

Members of the body of Christ enjoy protection within that body. The church confers protection from the malice of Satan. We are not immune from his assaults, but neither are we naked and helpless before them. He can attack, but he attacks us as members of an opposing army, the army of the victorious Christ. To be delivered to Satan means that we no longer march in rank. Instead we are isolated and exposed so that this protection is withdrawn. But to what end are we exposed? A disciplined member is exposed to "the destruction of the flesh, that his spirit may be saved in the day of the Lord Jesus."

Destruction of the flesh? What exactly does Paul mean? Is Satan going to be given leave to kill the poor man? Some scholars think so, though it is difficult to see how his death would save his spirit. Paul's meaning seems to be quite different. He uses the term *flesh* to mean carnality, the sinful nature that plagues us all. If the offender's carnal attitude is corrected he will have no anguish to face at Christ's judgment seat.

It is true that there are examples of disciplinary and of providential death in Scripture. Ananias and Sapphira paid for their sin with their lives. Yet as we saw in chapter five, their death was designed to awaken fear of a holy God in the infant church. On the other hand, "Sometimes God does take away the lives of His own people to prevent them from incurring further guilt," writes John Owen. "First, in the coming of some great temptation and trial upon the world, God knows that certain believers could not hold out against it, and thus would dishonour him and defile themselves. Isaiah 57:1 declares, 'The righteous is taken away from the evil to come.' Second, God takes away those who persist in ignorance of God's mind and will. This seems to have been the case of Josiah (see 2 Chronicles 35)."[2]

It is more likely, however, that Paul is thinking that the

Corinthian offender is to be disciplined so that a work of grace might be done in him. The only problem is to explain how handing a man over to Satan can accomplish a work of grace. Can Satan deal with a man's carnality?

Yes, he certainly can. His malicious darts hurt. Christians in pain cry out to God, often in fear and repentance. "Yet thou didst bring up my life from the Pit," cried Jonah, "out of the belly of Sheol" (Jon 2:6; 2:2). In the Corinthian case the measure worked. It has done so in many cases. While it is true that offenders ejected from the local congregation may become embittered and plunge further into sin, it is also true that others discover the disenchant-ment and miseries of sin. These in turn can awaken a hunger for true spiritual consolation and fellowship, especially if the offender left a church flaming with true koinonia, warmed by a faithful, loving Christian fellowship. Cold is never so cold as when you begin to recall the fires of home.

A Hierarchy of Sins?
The sin in Corinth was flagrant, the kind of sin which might be featured in modern tabloids. "Prominent Church Member Enjoys Incest." But as we have seen already, the sin arose from a particular church context, and it is the state of the church that bothers Paul more than the sin of the offender. It is as though the subheading in the tabloid might have read, "Church Leaders Insist, 'Tough Love Is What Matters.' "

How does one decide what calls for "handing over to Satan"? When does a sin become bad enough for so extreme a measure? Murder, incest and grand larceny are one thing, but where do we stop?

In verse 11 Paul could almost be construed as giving us a list. "I wrote to you not to associate with any one who bears the name of brother if he is guilty of immorality or greed, or is an idolater, reviler, drunkard, or robber—not even to eat with such a one." But Paul's purpose is not to give a list. Notice the unevenness of the list and the absence of definitions. How bad does the immor-ality have to be? Surely there are all grades of sexual sin from lustful thoughts (which Jesus equated morally with adultery) to sexual crimes. Where does one make the dividing line?

Again why do items like greed and verbal abuse appear alongside immorality and idolatry? Incest we can understand. But greed? It is sinful, true. But does it call for handing someone over to Satan? If lists were intended to guide us, the terms on the list would have come with carefully framed definitions. And the approach to church discipline would have to shift from seeking reconciliation to assessing the degree of legal guilt. It would be a highroad to legalism.

No, Paul is merely tossing out examples of everyday sins of *unchurched* non-Christians to show the absurdity of mixing apples and oranges. Church members and the unconverted unchurched cannot be treated in the same way because they are in very different situations and have had widely differing experiences. The unchurched unbelievers have not experienced the grace of a pardoning God or the fellowship of his people.

Nothing Paul says contradicts the principles we already discussed in Matthew where the nature of the sin is not even mentioned. It is also tragic that many churches seem to feel that *only* sexual sins call for reconciling discipline. In Matthew and in Corinthians the real offense is not the sin itself, but *compromising with* sin.

No, if we look at the context of the discussion (1 Cor 5:9-13), we see at once that the distinction Paul is trying to make is not that between sins calling for excommunication and sins to be tolerated. He is distinguishing between our treatment of Christian sinners and non-Christian sinners. We rub shoulders every day with swindlers, adulterers and people dabbling with the occult. Jesus went so far as to seek such people out to deliver them from darkness. While we are called to be separate from sin, we are to be seekers of the lost.

The case of the Christian offender is different. He must now experience the alienation he has chosen. He must learn *and the church must learn* that Christian fellowship means a whole lot more than hobnobbing with the saints. It means sharing together the righteousness of Christ, knowing communion in the spiritual joys and battles of daily living.

These are truths we must sometimes learn through pain. The offender learns by shock and isolation. He learns from the exposure of being cut off. Church members learn through the heart searching involved in the whole procedure. They are brought face to face with God's standards and forced to stand with him or against him. They are faced with the misery and resentment of the rejected offender.

The list is merely Paul's way of making sure that the Corinthians do not construe his remarks to mean that all sinners are to be avoided. As for Christian offenders, once the time for expulsion from the fellowship has come, it has to be complete ("not even to eat with such a one," 1 Cor 5:11).

So where does this leave us in regard to sins that call for discipline? As church members we begin with a dictionary load of sinful tendencies—laziness, gluttony, alcoholic overindulgence, greed, unbelief, prayerlessness, unkindness, a combination of secretiveness and gossip, materialism, vanity, pride, neglect of our spouses and families, wrong ambitions, a host of harmful habits, critical spirits, grumbling spirits, grouchiness, lack of Christian openness, manipulative tendencies, petty deceits, white lies, black lies, spite, con artistry, sexual lusts, selfishness, irresponsibility, fantasy lives—and so we could go on endlessly. They are the tendencies and "small" sins which, left unchecked, lead to serious trouble.

We are to train one another in godliness through corrective action *at the point where one or more of these becomes evident in a way which hampers mutual fellowship.* We help one another in the spirit of Matthew 18:15. And if help is stubbornly and willfully rejected, the sin (as we have been trying to make it clear) becomes the sin of turning one's back on God and his people.

Some specific forms of sin will be dealt with in part three. But we will not be taking time to treat them in detail because they are more sinful than others, but because of special, practical difficulties they lead to, which create special, practical problems. Here we are trying to look at the biblical principles themselves. But let us return to the gulf we are to create between ourselves and willfully sinning Christians.

The Dreadful Sentence

We have not used the word *excommunication* because of its many associations, but in the literal sense of the term Paul is talking about excommunication. In fact, both the Corinthian and the Matthew passages go much further than mere disbarment from participation in church activities. Social isolation is implied by the expressions used in both passages. Painfully extreme as this may seem, the implication is unavoidable. "Let him be to you as a Gentile and a tax collector" (Mt 18:17). "Let him who has done this be removed from among you. . . . You are to deliver this man to Satan for the destruction of the flesh. . . . not even to eat with such a one. . . . Drive out the wicked person from among you" (1 Cor 5:2, 5, 11, 13). These phrases describe extreme measures, measures that seem to express attitudes we warned against in the previous chapter. The offender may so perceive them. Nevertheless they are not in themselves inconsistent with love, and church members must continue to show love in whatever ways they can. (We saw an example of this in the case of Jack's story and will see it in Joe's story in chapter eleven.)

The pain can be greatest among families. And Christian families and churches react to these passages in a variety of ways. One church I know demands marital separation. Another family I know includes excommunicated and nonexcommunicated members. When the family gathers for supper they use two tables—tables that are neatly in line, not quite touching, but covered with one tablecloth. At one end of the ingenious arrangement sit the excommunicated members and at the other, the members still in fellowship! Somehow we must find our way among extremes which range between the horrendous and the absurd.

The Pain, the Tears and the Rejoicing

Paul did not enjoy writing to the Corinthians. "For I wrote you out of much affliction and anguish of heart and with many tears, not to cause you pain but to let you know the abundant love that I have for you" (2 Cor 2:4). True church discipline is no fun. The greater the love, the deeper the pain. Those who have not engaged in it have never experienced the pain. Nor have those who plunge into corrective church discipline as part of an internal power struggle. They are sublimely unaware of the hurt, the grief, the self-doubts, the tears, the hopes raised only to be dashed. Yet Paul had come to some kind of assurance in the matter. "For I felt sure of all of you, that my joy would be the joy of you all" (2 Cor 2:3).

Some make a fallacious contrast between the loving Jesus and the stern, hard and rigid Paul. But the matter of judgmentalism is just as abhorrent to Paul. No one liked conflict less. "Why do you pass judgment on your brother? Or you, why do you despise your brother? For we shall all stand before the judgment seat of God" (Rom 14:10). Again he writes, "We who are strong ought to bear with the failings of the weak, and not to please ourselves; let each of us please his neighbor for his good, to edify him. For Christ did not please himself" (Rom 15:1-3). The fact is that even some servants of God who try to be "loving" like Jesus and go out of their way to avoid conflict still find that when they preach and live the truth they unwittingly kick a hornets' nest because people perceive them as being "stern" like Paul.

Also consider how Paul warned them against overdoing it. "For such a one this punishment by the majority is enough; so you should rather turn to forgive and comfort him, or he may be overwhelmed by excessive sorrow. So I beg you to reaffirm your love for him. . . . Any one whom you forgive, I also forgive" (2 Cor 2:6-10).[3] He could trust their judgment in the matter because he knew what had happened in their hearts. "I rejoice," he writes, "not because you were grieved, but because you were grieved into repenting; for you felt a godly grief. . . . See what earnestness this godly grief has produced in you, what eagerness to clear yourselves, what indignation, what alarm, what longing, what zeal, what punishment! At every point you have proved yourselves guiltless in the matter" (2 Cor 7:9, 11).

With their forgiveness Paul perceived they now had discernment. If the matter was left too long Satan might do more than necessary. Irreversible despair might set in. Satan must not be allowed to gain unnecessary advantage (2 Cor 2:11).

You may remember Jack in chapter six. I asked him how he responded when the elders came to talk to him and invite him back to the fellowship. "I had to tell them, 'I don't know if I've really changed. I'm not sure I feel different inside.' "

"But you had?" I asked him.

Jack's eyes shone. "I've learned so much—it was incredible—all these new things about God . . ." His eyes filled with tears.

Extreme discipline does not always work. We don't carry it out because it works. We carry it out because Christ teaches us to carry it out, and we try to do so in the manner and in the spirit and with the aims he taught. But thank God it often does work. It will cost us love and pain. But when we see its fruits, we will weep for joy and lift our adoring hearts to the One who walked through pain and death to reconcile us to himself.

Part III
Practical Considerations

10
The Three Steps Reconsidered

SIN COMES TO LIGHT IN MANY WAYS. Whenever it does there is always a first step to be taken to correct matters.

"D'you mind if I ask your advice? It's about Jan Schmidt." Pete is consulting Mary Jane. "I hate to tell you this, but . . ."

Christ's injunction (remember Mt 18:15) demands that we go to the sinner once we know about a sin. This is step one. We go alone. We go without prior consultation with anyone. The matter at first remains solely between the two of us. In practice we fall down badly. By the time Pete asks Mary Jane for advice about Jan Schmidt, he may already have asked two other people. At least four people know about Jan's alleged misconduct. The gossip process is already well under way.

What should Mary Jane do? She should take Pete back to step

one. "Have you gone to her, Pete? You haven't? Then my advice is to go and talk to her right away."

In this chapter we will, to some extent, go over the ground we covered in chapter eight, but in this case repetition does little harm. Some points need extra hammering.

Step One
"Pastor, I wonder if you would talk to . . ."

Wise pastors learn the lesson quickly. "I am sorry to hear about what she did, Brenda. If you are right, the matter is certainly serious. But have you approached her about it? You haven't? You thought _I_ should be the one to tackle her? No, dear. That may come later. But Jesus makes it plain . . . I'll call you back about this later today."

My mother had a good technique. As the next-door neighbor filled her ears with the latest iniquities of the woman across the way, mother took her arm gently and said, "Come on, dear. Let's go and talk to her about it . . ."

We are dealing with the many varieties of gossip, in the world and in churches. Gossip is not always malicious. But gossip is multifaceted. It may come as a sanctimonious request for prayer or a pseudoconfession about my relationship with someone who bugs me. The subtleties are endless. Unknown to me, a group once spent weeks praying about sins they felt I was guilty of. I had been prayer-gossiped, prayer-judged and prayer-condemned long before I was approached. There are any number of ways of avoiding Jesus' simple command by some form of preliminary gossip. But in them all we evade our Christian duty.

In chapter eight we ruled out asking advice from others before confronting an offender. Perhaps we should modify our stand. Advice can be helpful. But names are unnecessary when you ask advice. Indeed there should be no clues, no hints.

We gossip for many reasons, for malice, for the sense of power we get, but sometimes because we are afraid, afraid of confrontation. We are afraid of the animosity we may encounter, or of the imaginary argument we may lose. We fear to make fools of ourselves. We have gone over the matter in our heads a dozen times, and there seems to be no painless way of dealing with the issue. We yearn for support, for someone who will see our side.

See our side? Isn't that the crux of the difficulty? Once we have begun to look for understanding from someone, we have already adopted the wrong perspective. Our primary goal is no longer to re-establish a broken relationship. Indeed there may never have been a relationship to break. So before we are ready to take the first step, we have some confessing to do, some request for divine aid in removing a log that has lodged itself (with miraculous painlessness) in our eye.

"Lord, I need your help. I thought I loved John, but perhaps I don't. I grow angry inside when I think of talking to him about this, angry when I think about what he did. I can't handle talking to him about it. I have fantasies about what I say, and then what he says, and before I know what's happened my thoughts grow ugly. What can I do about it?"

And the response may come, "Perhaps you should tell him how you feel. You may love him more than you realize. In any case I love him, and I have enough love for the three of us. I'll come with you."

And by his Spirit he will. Talking to John will involve talking about yourself as well as about him. It may mean admitting you've been sore at him and that you're still struggling. Try to remember you may not see matters clearly. Leave a door open. "John, when you said you didn't care . . . I felt, I still feel you meant you didn't care what happened to me. Was I wrong?"

The matter may be infinitely more serious but the principles remain the same:

1. Be open before God about your struggle.

2. Admit your struggle to your brother or sister and ask him or her to help.

3. Remember that you may not see things correctly yourself. You may have been thin-skinned or paranoid and have a distorted picture.

4. Don't beat about the bush. Get right to the point.

5. Be sure that reconciliation is your first (though not your only) goal.

Exceptions to the Rule?

We insisted that the rule about going *first* to an alleged offender is a rule that should never be broken. Difficulties arise where sexual sin is involved.

Case 1: Nick (not his real name) was one of several leaders in a house church. One day he was drawn into sex-play with a woman whose home he entered. During a second call he resisted her attempts to seduce him, but she followed him out of the house into his car where they "mixed it up a bit." As he drove away the woman's husband arrived and noted the man's license plate number. By a ruse he obtained Nick's telephone number and called his wife, instructing her to tell Nick to "keep off my woman."

Nick's wife told Nick about the telephone call, but he firmly denied what had happened. What was she to do? She *had* approached her husband but was far from satisfied with his response. So she called the elders of her church.

In the presence of his wife Nick was confronted with her story. He initially clung to his denial but later admitted what had happened. The elders were able to discuss in detail with him the dishonesty involved, the question of trust in the marriage and the possible consequences had the incident not come to light. As the group talked on, it became evident that marriage counseling from one of the counselors in the church was needed. The matter was not discussed publicly. The couple agreed to the counseling, and Nick was suspended from his position as a house-church leader.

Case 2: Carl, an older Christian, a natural leader and a soul-winner (but one who had no official position in his southern U.S. church), took a recently converted female member on a weekend trip. During the trip he tried but failed to seduce her. The girl told another girl in the church and both planned to confront him together. However, they first decided to check with elders in the church.

The elders decided that one of their own number should approach the man, seek to convince him of the harm done to a newly converted girl and make him aware of the dismay and hurt experienced by the elders. One elder felt the matter should be brought to the attention of the church as a whole since he saw Carl as a menace in the group. It was decided such a measure was not necessary.

Confronted, Carl openly admitted his wrong and made a full apology. He likewise expressed his repentance and apologies to the girl. He recognized that he had been operating "too autonomously" and needed to be more open, particularly with other men in the fellowship. He accepted the recommendation to be more involved in a house group.

What can we learn? First, a wrong had been committed and a state of alienation existed. A subsequent meeting in private was feared by the girl and was fraught with danger for both. They could perhaps have met in a public place, but the girl's confiding in her friend can readily be understood.

Second, whether the elder who approached Carl should have taken the girl along with him is perhaps open to question.

Lastly, while many people would share the misgivings of the elder who saw Carl as a menace in the church, we think the decision not to "go public" was correct. However, the decision involved spiritual discernment as to the reality of Carl's repentance. Our view is that it is impossible to make decisions of this sort without running risks, and that for too long churches have been motivated in their decisions by fear and by a need to protect their reputations. More commonly yet, churches run away from the problem by making no decision.

The Deceiving Heart

We all have a deceiving heart. We are all at times its victim. We may say we are acting in love, that our motive is reconciliation. We may actually believe ourselves when deep down our real need is to vindicate ourselves, to punish someone else, even to avenge ourselves of supposed wrongs.

Ken Blue and I have seen this happen too often to be naive about the ease with which the problem is going to be solved. But if we honestly want the Holy Spirit's illumination, we will have it. It is wanting it that counts, wanting it badly enough to endure his scrutiny of us, his determination to remove logs from our eyes that we may see clearly to deal with other people's faults. In corrective church discipline, motive is all important. We must go as reconciled reconcilers, newly purged and reconciled anew.

I have deceived myself about my motives in approaching someone (though my commonest self-deception is about my reasons for *avoiding* a confrontation). I have also known the pain of being attacked in the name of love when my accuser, as far as I could judge, was self-deceived.

Recently I received a letter from a man accusing me of "sinning against" him. We had had one or two (for me) painful encounters in the past, all of which, to my knowledge, had been satisfactorily resolved. The only "sin" I could think of was that I had failed to visit him when I paid a brief visit to his community. The reason for my neglect could well have been a fear of further unpleasant-ness. I wrote a letter apologizing for my discourtesy.

By return mail there came a letter bearing a lot of postage. It came by registered mail and special delivery. Inside the envelope were two pages of crowded typescript which could be summarized as follows:

1. The letter was written in love to save my soul from the flames of hell. The man's heart turned "over in grief before God" for me.

2. I was pretending not to know what my "real" sin was because of my inner deceit. (The "sin" and "sins" were not specified in the letter, however.)

3. The Holy Spirit had left me and I was under Satan's control.

4. Unless I came to see him "in accordance with Matthew 18:15" and in obedience to Matthew 5:22-23, the letter would be his "last communication to [me] here on earth."

5. The letter was signed, "In the love of Jesus."

I could be wrong (I did go to see him) but my feeling is that the man was deceived about his love. One of us was deceived. The principal lesson for me is that we both needed the wisdom of others. Hence one of the values of witnesses. I suggested as much, but my friend strenuously opposed the idea.

The example is an extreme one. It may help us to understand the spirit that inspired the Inquisition, the same spirit that also caused Zwingli to encourage civil authorities to murder Anabaptists. It may also help us to understand why throughout history church discipline has sometimes been so destructive instead of healing and restorative.

Yet is it so unusual? Are we not all, Christian though we may be, subject to like passions? Should it not serve as a warning about the ease with which our frustration and our deceiving hearts can mislead us? For we must be careful not to conclude that the author of the letter was unusually evil. I believe he dearly loved Christ. After all, as we already mentioned, did not the saintly Bernard of Clairveaux indulge in similar rages and persecutions?

The brother had probably failed to perceive his own heart. He professed to be able to discern the evil in mine. But this is unwise. Actions are one thing. Inner motivation is another. Many psychiatrists and psychologists would say he was *projecting* attitudes he himself harbored toward the person he accused, attitudes that had gained control of his consciousness, blinding him to his real motives.

Denial of Sin or Personality Clash?

In chapter eight we did not discuss how to proceed when the confrontation is unsatisfactory, that is, when fellowship is not restored, when matters instead of improving actually get worse, or when there seems to be a surface patching up which brings about no true reconciliation.

On the one hand, there is the danger of a legalistic one-two-three. One, I came and you didn't listen so now I'm going for my witnesses. Two, we came and you didn't listen so now we'll get you with step three. On the other hand, there is an equal danger of bending over so far backward that we opt for peace-at-any-price, forgetting that reconciliation has a cost. Sin, if there is sin, must be dealt with. Godly reconciliation is based always and only on canceled sin.

But is it a matter of sin? Or is it a matter of hurt feelings and misunderstanding? Often the matter is cleared up very quickly, even when the issue is one of incompatible personalities rather than what we normally speak of as sin, and even when the approach is a little rough. Years ago in Bolivia my wife, finding a fellow missionary grated on her, said to him one day, "Les, for some reason I just can't stand you!"

"Well, that's strange," Les replied. "I have exactly the same feeling about you."

When I came across them a few minutes later they were kneeling together confessing to God their mutual resentment. And from that day on they became the warmest of friends. It is a pity matters cannot always be resolved so simply.

We could say, of course, that the solution here lay in the openness the two displayed. But openness is a two-edged weapon. It can be a dagger that stabs just as easily as a knife that cuts through tangled irritations. Once when I gave a talk to a house group on Matthew 18:15, one young woman promptly made the rounds of the group venting spleen she had been holding against several other members for weeks. Reconciliation did not follow.

No doubt sin is always present in personality clashes and mutual irritations. But once we start thinking about corrective church discipline, we may begin to take ourselves (rather than sin) seriously. A simpler approach might be better. "Jan, we seem to have a hard time getting along. Sometimes I think it's your fault, but I can see I must get on your nerves at times. Think we can solve it? We may have to work at it, but could we begin by praying about it?" And ideally the encounter should be face to face. Letters, documents, telephone calls keep the other person at a distance. We avoid being fully vulnerable.

We wish we could give some magic formula. We can say the obvious, that both need to be open to the Holy Spirit, but often there is no simple solution but to recognize that if someone gets on my nerves, I too must have a problem. I knew a missionary who used to talk about the "saint perfecters" among us. His exegesis may not have been sound, but he had a point. He felt that certain irritating Christians were sent by God among us to act as sandpaper on our rough edges. They were "for the perfecting of the saints"!

We need wisdom to distinguish between irritation arising from our own personality quirks, the cultural and social differences of our fellow Christians (perhaps beams in our eyes do irritate after all!) and sin in their lives. And the distinctions are not always clear.

Unresolved Sin

But let us suppose you are dealing with a fellow Christian you suspect of theft, lying divisiveness, unkindness, malicious gossip or the like. You like the person and are troubled. Perhaps the person is someone you have led to Christ yourself, which will make the matter both easier in one sense and more difficult in another. You present your view of the matter and the thing turns sour. Your friend becomes angry, defensive, resentful and even tells you to mind your own business.

Anger, resentfulness and defensiveness are common (though carnal) reactions all of us are subject to. They are the kind of reactions God consistently reacted to with patience and longsuffering, both throughout biblical history and in every one of our lives. And what God has given to us, we owe to our brothers and sisters.

Therefore, our first response should be to be as patient as possible. We must do all we can to avoid getting into a verbal battle, making every allowance for resentfulness and defensiveness. The worst kind of thing to say is, "Now you're getting angry about it!" Or, "There's no need to get so huffy. I came in love, and if *this* is the way . . ." and so on.

If the "mind your own business" theme comes up, you must point out gently but firmly that it *is* your business. If you are going to be helpful, you will need to know the truth. Again, your need to know the truth arises because the person you are going to is a brother or sister in Christ. And fellow Christians are to care for one another's spiritual as well as physical well-being.

If he accuses you of being no better than he, admit it without any qualification. You are not approaching Jim because you are better than Jim. If the positions were reversed, you hope Jim would do for you what you are trying to do for him.

So take time. Make allowances. And above all, encourage Jim to do most of the talking. Do so by being genuinely interested in and understanding of his feelings. Chances are he'll talk himself into a better frame of mind once he is able to talk and will be better able to admit his faults.

The art of listening is crucial. Resist your yearning to win an argument. Listen with the intent of understanding. Let him know by your silences and by your sympathy to his needs that you come as friend rather than foe. Silences and grunts of understanding communicate love far better than pious protestations of it. And usually it is when the genuineness of your care dawns on Jim that his resistance will break down, and he will be relieved to get his sin off his chest. His conscience had been working all along. The Holy Spirit had seen to that. What he needed all the time was an understanding listener.

In this way you could very well gain your brother. You will have gained him without a need for steps two and three. True, there may be some further cleaning up to be done in the form of confessions, apologies and restitutions to other persons. But the main point we want to get across is that there is no need to proceed to step two simply because step one should prove hard. You should be prepared to see Jim several times if necessary.

Step Two
But Jesus plainly anticipated that success would not always attend step one. With the best will in the world things go wrong. Stubborn hearts refuse to yield. Denials, lies and rebellion may resist the loving process of reconciliation. Is this not typical of the history of God's dealings with his people?

So we call in the witnesses. Who are they? In some cases the selection will be fairly obvious. Names may have been named. "So-and-so will *prove* that I said this, or was in such a place on such a night." At least one member of the sex of the person facing accusation should be present. A woman accused of sexual sin should not be left facing a set of male witnesses. Other witnesses may be wise and godly Christians whose reliability and wisdom have been tested by years of faithfulness. Pastors (poor, over-worked pastors!) may or may not be necessary. Often they can use a break from hassles. And in any case they may have a more important role to play later.

Now the aim in approaching the offender along with witnesses will be the same aim that prompted the first approach. We are not out to nail a sinner but to rescue him or her. The goal is mercy not condemnation. But it must be mercy on the basis of truth and of confessed sin—if sin there is. (Remember, the accuser may be wrong.) But sin, if it clearly is sin, must be faced.

Simplicity and plainness of speech is kinder than elaborate attempts at kindness which take the form of beating around the bush. Remember, the accused is likely to feel ganged up on. Clean wounds heal more quickly than repeated clumsy scratches. The original friend could begin by saying something like: "Jim and I are having a problem. I suspect he's been helping himself to the offering plate. He says he hasn't. I'd like to accept his word because we've been pretty close. Problem is that only the two of us have access to the offering plates, and the totals don't tally with the amounts on the outside of the envelopes. Maybe you guys could help us sort it out."

Hopefully, someone will at this point say, "OK, Jim. Let's hear your side of the story." And from that point on, the same patience, the same desire to understand both Jim and his accuser must prevail. Rebuke and sternness may be needed, but truth can also become plain without hassling.

The witnesses are in one sense part jury, part defense lawyers. Truth must be discovered, but what is the truth? Could there be some other explanation of the discrepancy? Could any practical steps be taken to check on some other hypothesis? But if all attempts to help lead inevitably to the conclusion that Jim has in fact been stealing, then the question becomes one of how to help Jim to come to genuine honesty with himself as well as with the group. And should this also fail, the third step may become the only alternative.

Step Three

Step three is to bring the matter before the local church. Remember that this is to be a purifying process for the church as well as for the sinner. Indeed, and we use the words soberly, "all hell" could break loose at this point. In previous chapters we saw how wrong attitudes in the church might have to be dealt with.

Should the sinner be present? His or her presence would not only be helpful but in everyone's (including the sinner's) best interests. In the following chapter we will look in detail at Joe's story. The elders asked him to confess his sin to the home church he had been involved with. Joe could have refused, but he decided instead to go along with the idea. Painful but ultimately beneficial results followed. Had Joe not followed the elders' suggestion, they would have had to do the dirty work themselves. They and the folk involved in counseling Joe would have had to make matters plain. The result would have cleared the air less satisfactorily than Joe's open confession.

But the sinners may refuse, and the church has no mandate to coerce them. The refusal to be present would constitute the sinner's rejection of the church's efforts at reconciliation. In the end the leaders may have to make a simple statement, call on the testimony of those involved in the case to answer questions and then let the church decide. But the decision of the majority may (as Roland Allen pointed out) prove to bring about the restoration of the sinner.

Because of a fear of trouble, many church leaders go to great lengths to avoid bringing a resistant sinner before the congregation as a whole. They default on step three. Rudy, the new assistant pastor of a large community church in New Jersey, recently presided over the marriage ceremony for a middle-aged couple, Doris and Chet (a deacon). Almost immediately another woman, Keri, approached the assistant pastor claiming she had sought to dissuade the couple from marrying because their marriage amounted to legalization of a previous bigamous relationship.

On checking the facts, Rudy discovered that Chet was newly divorced and had for many years commuted to work in a town two hundred miles away, spending the weekends at home with his first wife, but living during the week with the woman he subsequently married. On being transferred to his "weekend" town, he promptly divorced his "weekend" wife.

Rudy wished both to absolve his complicity in what he saw as sin and to help Chet and Doris to see and repent of what they had done. He was unclear about the proper course the couple should take, but saw that the issue could not be left unresolved. He approached them along with his informant, but was thrown out of the couple's house and told to mind his own business.

He then approached Arthur, the senior pastor, who told him in alarm that neither he (the senior pastor) nor the church would "touch this thing with a barge pole." What at this point was Rudy's responsibility? Ought he to drop the matter or take further action? If further action was his duty, what was that action to be?

Different people give different answers with different reasons. In our opinion Rudy could not morally forget about the matter. Once he had approached Arthur, he was faced with a double problem. Sin in the church was compounded and confounded by the senior pastor's cowardly negligence. While he would be wrong to defy his boss's authority, he had a duty to draw Arthur's attention to his failure. Hopefully Rudy would entreat rather than rebuke, seeking reconciliation with the senior pastor on a matter about which both felt deeply but over which they disagreed.

And if no reconciliation could be secured, it would be Rudy's duty to bring others to help convince Arthur of his wrong. The most obvious source of help in such a church would be the church board. However, some senior pastors, more experienced in church politics and less idealistic than younger men, can and do outmaneuver them. And many church boards are made up of people who would instinctively take sides for reasons other than those of dealing with sin and bringing about godly reconciliation. Should no resolution come by this step, we believe the assistant pastor should seriously consider resigning from the church because of his leadership position.

It is impossible to prescribe an ideal course for every situation. Church constitutions and bylaws do not always lend themselves to biblical discipline. But every effort must be made to follow corrective action through to completion.

Further questions concerning step three arise. What is the whole church? When Jesus told the disciples to tell the church about a matter, did his words imply that the matter should be brought before a congregation of five thousand?

Two principles that must be kept in mind are those of gossip and church purity. We must avoid gossip and we must promote church purity. The two factors are intimately related. Where church members are already gossiping, a clear statement of the truth can do much to take the spice out of the gossip, particularly one so worded that it rebukes self-righteous gossips. Church impurity often consists in judgmental and divisive attitudes gossiped among church members. But where church members have no knowledge of a disciplinary matter, perhaps being unacquainted even with the persons involved, we open an occasion for gossip by announcing it.

First-century churches were largely small house churches. Numbers were probably small by modern standards. People almost always knew one another well. Thus the church Jesus referred to was the small unit where everything would probably be known anyway. In such a setting a disciplinary matter that is resisted is _de facto_ a community matter. Therefore it would seem best to interpret Christ's words "to the church" to refer to the particular subgroup with which the offender associates most, if such a group exists. This would avoid exposing the offender to unnecessary humiliation.

A further problem concerns a Christian's responsibility to a sinning friend who belongs to another church. Does one have the right to "discipline" a brother who does not belong to your church, who falls as it were under someone else's jurisdiction? Jurisdiction, however, is not always relevant. I once came across two men fighting flames in their truck on a lonely road equidistant from two municipalities. The police in both told me when I telephoned them that it did not "fall within their jurisdiction." The plight of the men trying to avert an explosion seemed unimportant to them.

The point of the parable of the good Samaritan is that we are to be neighbor to whomever we can, to do good wherever possible, to heal whomever we find wounded, to turn sinners from the error of their ways and above all to be peacemakers or reconcilers. However, if the person we are helping does not want help, clearly matters of jurisdiction become more important. Steps two and three will concern his or her own church. Help of this kind should be sought in that setting. And if the church refuses to respond, then in our judgment, the matter of further disciplinary steps should be set aside.

Pastors and Counselors

Another problem concerns confidentiality. Confidentiality is the *norm,* not only for people identified as Christian counselors, but for every Christian. But there comes a point when confidentiality defeats the counselor's aims, and in addition hinders the greater good of church discipline. When counselors have a client's best interests in mind, and stop thinking about their "relationship with" a client (which often boils down to a counselor's neurotic and sinful need to have a client go on liking him or her), they will realize this is so. Godly, experienced counselors make such issues clear at an appropriate point in their counseling. Early in their discussions with clients, they should explain that certain kinds of information cannot be kept confidential, such as a case where the welfare of the community overrides the privacy of the individual. Otherwise, confidentiality becomes complicity with sin. This represents humanist, not Christian, thinking.

All that remains, as we mentioned in chapters eight and nine, is for the terrible sentence to be pronounced. Our only and urgent reminder is that redemptive contact be maintained with the sinner.

But the question may be asked, what has been the role of the pastor, the elders, the deacons in all this? Earlier in the chapter we indicated that in step one the pastor's role was educative. It was his duty to teach a telephone gossip that she had a duty to perform, and that it was his duty to see that her duty was carried out. Obviously by the time the matter is brought to the church as a whole, the church leadership will know what is going on, even if they have not been involved in step two.

It is here that leaders' roles as teachers, guides, moderators are vital. Such meetings are not usually either smooth or pleasant. Nor should we aim at making them so. They can be silent but pregnant with unspoken hostilities. Usually, as we have already pointed out, attitudes among the membership have begun to form, and if discretion has prevented them from forming before the meeting, they will certainly form during it. Members with strong feelings should be admonished to express opinions and to ask questions, but to do so constructively and not bitterly. The role of the spiritual leadership will be identical to that of Paul in 1 Corinthians, one of teaching and instructing the congregation in their attitudes, their duties and in the basic issues of what has taken place.

Confidentiality? The time for confidentiality is ended. The matter has become one of rejection of the mercy of God's people. And in any case, as we have already made clear, nothing kills gossip like a full and open discussion of all the facts.

Is the Church Infallible?
But what if the offender has really been innocent all along? What if a terrible travesty of justice is being carried out? It has happened in the past, and it can happen in the future. There is no way to guarantee it will not happen; and the less experienced the church in these matters, the greater is the likelihood of a miscarriage of justice.

It sounds cold to say that without running such risks corrective church discipline will not take place. Hopefully, the accused can expect more help and justice than can those judged in civil and criminal courts, where the Holy Spirit's direction is commonly lacking. Yet would it be right to do away with civil and criminal courts because errors are made? Clearly not. Still less should we withhold the incalculable value of corrective church discipline from the church for fear we will make a mistake. All we can do is cast ourselves on God, whose concern for the offender is much greater than our own.

The experience is more likely than not to be a learning experience for all whose cost in personal pain will be more than worth the eventual result of a truly disciplined church. But it raises the matter of the accountability of the church leadership which we will discuss more fully in chapter sixteen.

Another Church

Events may force matters. A common occurrence nowadays is for a disgruntled disciplinee to seek membership in a more congenial congregation, whose pastor will listen with a sympathetic ear and a growing indignation to what has happened. Nothing can be more flattering than for a pastor to be consulted by a hurt and wounded soul who has suffered at the hands of another church.

Some people argue that such church transfers render all discipline pointless. They don't. Even if they did, it would still be our duty to obey Jesus. We are to do as the Lord of the church commands. In any case if we define church discipline in terms of training we will see that training still benefits those who accept and profit by it.

So what should happen when an excommunicated person switches churches or even denominations? Some attempt should be made by the leadership of the two churches to get together, preferably with the offender. Such a meeting can be fruitless or fruitful. But the same attitude of a loving desire to help the offender, now combined with a concern for reconciliation between churches (and not merely an attempt to justify the first church's action) are basic prerequisites to a resolution.

I attended a meeting recently where elders grappled with an unresolved problem involving themselves and another church. Two members from the elders' church, Tom and Jeanette, were sleeping together while dating. When the matter came to light the elders sought to confront and counsel the couple, but Tom left in anger for another part of the country. There he attended a church whose pastor, Bill, knew the elders of Tom's previous church. Tom told Bill his story, received counsel from him and was accepted into fellowship.

Jeanette, on the other hand, seemed to accept the counsel the elders gave her. She agreed to break off the connection. Letters from Tom continued to arrive. Some of these, which were subsequently found, contained both lascivious suggestions to her and expressed hostility and contempt for the leadership of her church. Ultimately, Jeanette continued the contact with Tom clandestinely by mail and telephone, joined him and received counseling along with him by Bill. They were soon married.

Once married, they returned to their original city and requested membership of their first church. Their dishonest tactics were brought to their attention, as well as Tom's letters, which had expressed contempt for the leadership. He had also lied slander-ously (according to the statements in his letters) to Bill, who had (again, according to Tom's letters) accepted his statements and viewpoint. The elders asked only that he correct his slanderous statements to the other church and, since they had little reason to trust him, to let them see the letter he sent. The letter, which they allowed me to see, was a curious blend of flattery to Bill and acknowledgment of the righteous judgment of the elders of his original church. As for correcting slanderous statements, Tom merely stated, "This may have manifested [by] blatant maligning, . . ." and, "If this maligning is true, . . . I want to apologize." Happily the matter ended well. Tom saw his weakness and repented. The couple are at the time of writing restored to fellowship.

In all this time, however, there had been no discussion or correspondence with Bill's church, even though he was on friendly terms with the leaders of the first church. The counseling and the marriage were clearly regarded by Bill as not being their business. John Owen argued that it was the duty of the receiving church in the case of "supposed maladministration of justice" to "inquire into the matter and take cognisance of it." Not to do so would harden believers in their sin and thus "frustrate the ordinance of Christ" and make a church that failed to inquire "among the enemies of Christ."[1] If he is right, and we believe he is, there are many, many churches frustrating "the ordinance of Christ" today.

No doubt discussion would be biased by different moral standards. But what better way to think about such differences than in a context of seeking unity over a practical issue? If the first church had acted wrongly, they could have been exposed to a different viewpoint.

Every effort should be made for a meeting of some sort. If possible, the meeting should be face to face, where preferably both sets of leaders, witnesses and the person being disciplined can be present together. If the person who is being or has been disciplined is unwilling to be present at such a meeting, the second church may have pause for thought. Clearly the situation has equal possibility both for unpleasantness and for glorious healing. But feelings always begin to modify when we look at one another's faces. Imagination gives place to reality.

Unfortunately, Ken Blue and I have no actual experience of this type of encounter. Yet we urge that attempts be made to bring them about. The worst that could happen would be that two estranged churches would remain estranged. But is God dead? The high payoff could very well be the purification of two churches, a new fellowship and the deliverance of sinners.

11
Joe's Story

JOE'S STORY WAS WRITTEN SPONTANEOUSLY. I may have been the first person to read it. He gave me permission to use it in any way I wished. I have condensed it, clarified one or two sentences, and changed names and other information to protect identities. Otherwise, here it is, as Joe wrote it.

Up from the Pit

My sojourn with God goes way back to when I was a child. My mother and father did not have a stable relationship. I remember seeing my father beating my mother's head against one of the closet doors. I was about two years old at the time and this type of thing was to go on for about ten more years. And it got more brutal as it went on.

My first encounter with the idea of God and Christ was in a summer mission school taught by some Benedictine sisters and

Oblate fathers at a Catholic Church in a small city in California. Since I began to identify more with my mother, her pains, her way of life (one devoted to her family and to Christ) the Church also became important to me. I became an altar boy and had the Latin Mass memorized by the time I was six. The idea of being one of *God's* children was most appealing to me as I didn't feel secure with my family life.

I remember feeling real special when I was baptized in water when I was about five. I remember looking in the mirror to see if any physical change had occurred. But at the same time as my awareness of God began, there began also a problem that was to haunt me for many years.

One of my sisters seduced me. I remember feeling very guilty. This went on infrequently for about six years, until I was eleven or twelve. Even though I stopped, it left me scarred. I learned how to be around God and his church and not to reveal this to anyone. I learned how to turn my conscience off and on at will. I had to so I could stop feeling guilty.

Also about the age of ten I stole some money from my mother's purse. When asked about it I lied. Then I did it again and again, and each time it got easier. I remember feeling extremely guilty and being afraid to confess it to the priest. Thus I learned how to lie and be deceitful at a very young age.

My mother died on January 2, 1973. During her last illness I was reaching the height of my rebellion against her. I had started cutting school and goofing around with my friends and, of course, lying to her about it. Because I saw her suffer so much on my account as she tried to keep the family together, it was very frustrating to lie to her. So I would get angry and resentful when she confronted me. When she died, I became overwhelmed with guilt. So I decided to "take a break" from God, to sin and to live the carefree life I never had the liberty to do when my mother was around. Since she supplied the motivation for me to do good, I saw no reason to continue.

I developed a science for manipulating girls, almost all of whom were willing to go to bed with me. I remember having to force myself not to listen to my conscience, not to care, to appear cool.

I got into every kind of drug and the drug subculture, "Chico-power" style. I became friends with my lifelong arch enemies and soon became a leader. We all packed guns and knives and talked big. Then I got into dealing drugs and into violence. I remember going home to sleep and feeling more and more afraid of God, but still not caring. By this time, I couldn't blame my childhood for my sins and bad patterns because I was making conscious decisions daily to do what I knew to be wrong.

For a year and a half after graduation I worked for my father and was very successful as a salesman, but I grew tired of the long hours, with drugs and sex as my only stimulation. Then I began to remember God again. I started going to church regularly, carrying the baggage of my sins. I asked a priest friend how to become a priest. I said I wanted to try. Before I knew it, I was at the college seminary. I was disillusioned. I had expected to find a monastery, but I found a loose college, full of sinners, with God nowhere in sight.

With the help of Father José Lopez Bongarrá I opted to stay and see it through. But the old sins came and found me. Following graduation I opted to leave the seminary, having learned only academic excellence and secret sin in the Catholic Church. I knew I had not progressed spiritually because I was still enslaved to my lustful passions.

During my senior year I met a girl (I'll call her Joan) who introduced me to a Christian house fellowship. Our relationship didn't work out, as neither of us could maintain it on a Christian level. It showed me how immature I was. But this was only the tip of the iceberg.

So for about seven months I went for Christian counseling and tried to become more involved in the house fellowship. Then I met another girl, decided to date her, and quickly became sexually involved. Here is where God started to tell me that he was no longer going to tolerate the deceitfulness and immorality of my life. Why? Because now I knew about grace, about walking in the Spirit and about the prerequisites of spiritual leadership.

For seven months I had led people to believe I was spiritual. Although some sensed I was faking it, the majority were willing to give me the benefit of the doubt. Then one day my closest and dearest friend told me that I was going to be asked to become a home-church leader. This was to me a great honor, but one I knew God didn't want me to accept under false pretenses. So I did something I was highly unaccustomed to doing, that is, to expose myself completely in all my wickedness to some of the leaders.

I realized that I had gotten so good at sinning and deceiving people that hardly anyone could detect my rebellion. So it was either a matter of going deeper and deeper in rebellion to God, or expose myself, accept the consequences and try to find some integrity. My closest friend was deeply hurt. He had done all he could to disciple me.

I was told that I could not become a house leader or teach in public, and must not date until I had truly repented and shown some progress. But I was treated with grace and was told the whole church didn't have to know what had happened. I could also minister to whomever I had the opportunity to.

I was set back a little, but most of my grief was self-centered and brief. One of the elders told me it concerned him that I was not more worried about all I had done. I wasn't worried, so it didn't bother me. Somehow, though, I knew and felt my heart was still hard.

So for the next six months I went about ministering the best I knew how. I got to be pretty good, as I was in tune with the needs of our young church and was providing them with what they needed. With six fellows I met, I started a group Bible study. These guys became fairly close to me. But I didn't let them get close enough. I later told them of my sin tendencies and asked their help, but never really allowed them to help me.

It then became apparent to me that most of our church members were young in the Lord and needed some basic doctrine. So I started a class that was going to meet as many of their needs as possible. It went very well. I soon became attached to two girls. I started to work closely with them, and the leaders cautioned me about my sin tendencies. By this time I believed I had all the checks around me that were necessary to keep me from falling. A big mistake. As time went on I became less and less accountable to others and more and more involved with the two girls. Then my work with the boys started to suffer. I knew what was wrong but didn't want to face it. I needed to stop working with the girls.

Then came warnings from some of the elders to be careful, to stay away from Pam in particular, but by this time I had become infatuated with her. The more they told me to beware, the more time I spent with her. Other people also warned me and I told them things were under control, whereas in fact we had become physically involved.

I knew that if it persisted I would be severely disciplined, but somehow this didn't seem real to me. So Pam and I discussed it and decided to cut down our time together. By that time one of the elders *told* me to do so. I told him we had it all figured out and that we were going to start seeing each other only every Sunday beginning Sunday, August 7. I told him this on the preceding Monday. So Pam and I dated nightly for the next week.

Finally, Sunday came and just as we were leaving the coffee shop we decided "out of the blue" (or darkness, I should say) to get a room in a motel. Not once did I care about what this would do to my walk or hers, how all the other brothers and sisters would be affected, let alone how God felt about it. It was like being under a spell. I was convinced I could lie about it and with time get over it. So did Pam.

Monday evening came and with it my meeting with my two Christian counselors. They knew something was up because it was written all over me. One of them knew I had kissed Pam and asked me if I wanted to talk about it. He asked me if that was all. I refused to answer. The meeting ended and they went straight to Pam's. I knew that was where they would go. I didn't know what Pam would do, even though she had said she would not tell. So rather than put her through all that I called them there and asked them to come back.

They came and I told them. There was dead silence. One of them had pointed me out to the church the night before, saying I was someone who knew real compassion, and who loved him. They left dejected and hurt, in tune with the misery our home church was about to experience. I was panic stricken. I could only think of myself and the sins I had committed. So I went to search for Pam. I met her that night and the following day for lunch. In our confusion we discussed bizarre and absurd options. But on Tuesday evening (my twenty-fifth birthday) I was attending my last central teaching meeting until God would see fit for me to return to the church. I became more and more depressed. The horror of what I had done was now clear to me, and Satan was relentless as my Accuser. I was in the deepest, blackest pit I had ever experienced.

"My God," I thought, "I am so wicked and so, so sick in my heart. Just look at what I have done!" Yet I was numb, feeling nothing, not even remorse. But as I felt the Word being preached, it began to pierce my hard heart like a sword. Then another brother came, a brother who is very special to me, and whom God sent to help me in my condition.

He looked at me with the eyes of Christ, filled with compassion and hurt. He said to me, "You've gone and done it, haven't you?" Then he put his arm around me and said, "No matter what, I just want you to know that God still loves you, and so do I." This brought me to uncontrollable weeping. He went on to deliver the mightiest exhortation I have ever heard in my life. With the words of Christ he said, "So you've been dangling your toes over the pit and looking down and wondering how deep it is. And finally God said, 'I suppose I'll let Joe find out.' So now you're at the bottom of the pit and it's ugly and black. Learn your lesson and learn it well. But just remember God won't let you stay there, because he loves you and you're forgiven. He just wants you to find out what you've been playing around with. He caught you with your defenses down. Let me exhort you, brother! Don't ever take your armor off again! Put it back on! Don't give up! Don't run away!" And so he continued to exhort me, expounding Ephesians 6 vividly and powerfully. I will always love and cherish him, especially for his exhortation.

The saddest day of my life came on Thursday, August 11. The elders met with me. They told me they were burdened for me and believed I was sorry for my sins. But that was not enough. It had come to the point where they believed they could not help me, as I had exhibited to them an unwillingness to listen to them and to pay heed to their previous words of warning. This being so, how could they help me further? Moreover, they feared for the other sisters in the fellowship for whom they were responsible as shepherds of the flock.

They pointed out that Scripture instructs us to throw out people with this type of unwillingness. So until the Lord told them otherwise, they asked me to leave the fellowship, to go out into the world for the destruction of my flesh. But before I was to leave, they asked me to stand before my class to confess my sins and hear their reproofs, to which I agreed. I had left them no other choice. It really touched me when one of them at the end of the meeting hugged me and gently said, "Get well!"

Later came further humiliation. As one elder gave a brief explanation of church discipline and introduced my sin to the class, I stood before them and told them of my sin and the accompanying problem. As I looked into their eyes I saw horror, compassion, hate and bewilderment. After I concluded, much to my surprise most of them stood and told me how much I had helped them and how they were going to miss me. Others expressed how they felt ripped off personally, how much I was grieving the Holy Spirit and how much I had hurt the church.

It is a night I will never forget. These were people who trusted me, respected me and looked up to me for leading from God. And I had told them that for a few months of hurtful passion I had betrayed both Pam and them, and was willing to forfeit all I had built. I left in total humiliation. I spent the next few nights getting high on pot with new roommates. I felt sorry for myself and totally worthless. So why not act like it?

As I started praying I remembered that the elders had told me to really search for truth, to pray, read the Word and spiritual books, take walks, stay away from tempting situations, from women and from drugs. I knew I had never given up smoking pot, as I would do it every so often and not tell anyone.

So I asked myself, "Well, Joe, what do you *really* want to do in life? Do you want to go on lying and living a compromised life, or are you going to get serious. . . ?" I knew that this was where it started. After my first confession about sex and pot, I would go over to Terry's, get high and watch football in the fall. This started me over again in my deceitful ways, since I told the leaders I had done it twice but had stopped, whereas in fact I continued.

About this time I started reading the Gospel of Mark. In it I found two very convicting and inspiring verses. One was Mark 2:17, "Those who are well have no need of a physician, but those who are sick; I came not to call the righteous, but sinners." Boy did I feel like a complete, helpless sinner! Christ's words touched me. I thought that if Christ could heal the sick people he healed in Mark's Gospel, surely he could help me. And we could begin with having me stop smoking pot!

Mark 3:35 was the other verse that stood out: "Whoever does the will of God is my brother, and sister, and mother." I decided that I really wanted to do God's will and not smoke pot again. It had cost me too much. I had been smoking it for the previous ten years and as a result my conscience was getting seared. I had constantly opened the door to Satan, to his lies and accusations. Praise be to God I've been able to say no every day since then.

Then I started to search, plead, beg for God to give me the strength to obey him and to do his will. I spent many a moment begging in tears to be delivered from the temptation to give way to despair and to let panic overwhelm me. I needed to get to know God "for real." I would also go through periods of feeling totally alienated from God and from all that was important to me. I was a blind man groping in darkness, tossed around by one feeling after another. I would cry out, "My Lord, I know you will not forsake me, I know you're there, but where are you?" Yet as I would plead and weep the Lord would come to me gently and tenderly to comfort me until I fell asleep.

The friend who had exhorted me so powerfully was sent again to me by the Lord to tell me of a book he was reading, Charles Swindoll's *Three Steps Forward, Two Steps Back*. Desperate, I bought and read it, finding it spoke precisely to my needs, teaching me about waiting for God, about the futility of striving, and about the fact that life was a task rather than a trip. The book was probably one of the most critical points in changing my perspective of becoming God-focused. Thank you Lord for Charles Swindoll and his wonderful book!

Another book I read powerfully brought home to me the deceitfulness and sickness of my heart. I thought I had hit rock bottom before, but I now began to see my life riddled with deceit and my heart with sinful disease. The process was a long one. My first great lesson had been to learn of God's extraordinary grace to me in pardoning me freely and making me his child. My second was to understand that while I remained a son of Adam I now shared the life of the Son of God. A new heart and a new spirit had been born within me when I had become a believer, and the heart of stone had been taken away. God's Spirit was within me! The answer to Jeremiah 17:9-10 was Ezekiel 36:25-27.

I cannot explain in words how these truths became real to me. This second truth dawned on me around 9 A.M., September 18. As I was standing in the unemployment line reading Watchman Nee's *Normal Christian Life,* it hit me like a lightning bolt. I felt elated. I couldn't stop smiling. I thought my heart was going to jump out of my chest. The man behind me must have thought I had gone crazy. As soon as I left the unemployment desk I almost ran to the car, got inside and howled for joy! I went to the church office, trying to hide my feelings from the secretary, but she could see something had happened, and asked me what. So I told her. Later I shared my joy with one of the elders.

It cannot have been a coincidence that the meaning of these and many other Scriptures was opened up to me during the next few hours for on Saturday, September 20, I met with the elders again, having seen them a week before. They were convinced I was truly repentant and could see no valid reason for keeping me out of fellowship any longer. So they welcomed me back, giving me some disciplinary conditions:

1. I was to be completely accountable to all the elders for my behavior.

2. The elders reserved the right to confront or to question me about any area of my life which they might feel led to address.

3. Far from being free to date, I was not to spend any time

exclusively with any sister.

4. I was not to teach publicly.

5. I was to attend the home church of the elders' choice.

6. If I failed to abide by these restrictions or to act upon their directions, the elders reserved the right to exclude me from fellowship again.

7. The above measures were to remain effective until the elders were led to lift them.

8. I was to consider myself to be a member of different standing from the rest in that I was not yet granted the same freedom and trust accorded to other members.

I now find these conditions humiliating, but that is good because I need humiliation. And while they seem stiff, I have to agree that they are indeed fair. Also they are not merely control measures for me but are *protective* measures for the body; this is most understandable. I admit to myself here and now they are hard to swallow and will continue to be so for some time. But this is good in that it will force me to rely totally on God, looking to him for strength, emotional support, courage and respect. I want moral integrity in my life. I want to be scourged and molded.

Lord Jesus, thank you for bringing me thus far. Lord, I want to love you and I want to put what you have shown me in action; please help me, Lord, to do this. I still do and always will need you as much as ever.

Joe's Story in Retrospect

Joe's story raises questions and calls for comments in the following areas: (1) It illustrates something we universally underestimate—the power of sin in believers' lives. (2) It also illustrates the role of ordinary Christians in the broad training process of church discipline, as well as the Holy Spirit's timing, and his use of fallible Christian literature. (3) It raises questions about the role and the responsibilities of leaders and the severity of the measures adopted in Joe's case. Let me consider each of these three in turn.

First, sin is like having cancer, but refusing to see the doctor. We are afraid. We know but we don't want to know. So we hide from self-knowledge. We hope the cancer will go away, thus condemning ourselves to live in a world of anxiety-flavored fantasy while the cancer advances relentlessly.

Joe had been discipled. That is to say his Christian life had been subject to personal teaching, prayer and supervision by a brother in Christ. He had grasped the principle of divine grace and forgiveness of sin. He was regenerate. Yet there were depths in his heart that grace had not touched. He had learned how to deceive himself and others (have not we all?) from his earliest years. He had even, following his conversion, learned to be "open" and to ask for help, yet without letting anyone get close enough to give him the help he needed. There were areas in his heart he did not want to admit were there. He knew, yet he did not want to know. Moreover, he was perceptive enough to spot spiritual needs around him and minister to them effectively. He was perceptive enough and gifted enough to help others, but not enough to be honest with himself.

Hundreds of thousands of Christian workers are in the same boat. We belong to the church of the self-deceived. Jeremiah is right. Our hearts are deceitful *above all things*. Corrupt. *Desperately* so. Impossible to fathom (Jer 17:9). Yet God perceives their depths, and will deal with them in this life or the next. Happy is the man or woman who is delivered in this life from shame in the next.

The Gift of Helps
Second, Joe's story illustrates that ordinary church members play a powerful role in corrective church discipline, whether for good or ill. When Paul listed helps among various spiritual gifts (1 Cor 12:28), perhaps he meant a lot more than we normally suppose. The friend who exhorted Joe and gave him books played a significant role in his restoration.

The reactions of his Christian friends to his confession varied. Most were compassionate. Some were bitter. Yet if the confession (in this case to those immediately involved in his ministry) was right, and we believe it was, we must leave the consequences with God. Truth is not always welcome. There are those who would prefer to believe that all is well. It's like our denial of cancer all over again. What we don't know can't hurt us, at least not for the moment.

Lastly, several questions about leadership arise from Joe's story. First, we notice Joe's comment that the leaders felt they had done all they could before they proceeded with the final step. Joe agreed with them. When is it time for us to cry, "Enough is enough"? There are no easy answers. Younger spiritual leaders tend to be less patient, and usually err on the side of being too precipitous. But older leaders can be too hesitant. All of us are victims of our temperaments. Experience, prayer and fasting, the direction of the Holy Spirit are all of great importance in exercising judgment of this sort.

Second comes the question of the dual responsibility of leadership. The leaders were responsible for Joe. They were responsible for the flock. Joe was a wolf and the flock needed protection. To balance both responsibilities calls for the same sort of discernment that we discussed a moment ago. Some leaders are so scared of sexual sinners that they go overboard in protecting the flock. In actual fact they often are unconsciously protecting their own (the leaders') reputation. Clearly the leaders in Joe's church were aware of the need for balance and perspective.

The third comment concerns the fact that the leadership followed up on Joe. They continued to meet regularly with him. Why then (and here comes a fourth matter for discussion) were their restrictions so severe when Joe was received back into fellowship? Perhaps we would have to know more to be in a position to judge. We should notice that the restrictions were time-limited. Joe was not to remain a second-class citizen for ever. Joe himself saw them as appropriate and a protection for him, though he did not enjoy them. In any case their severity need not imply coldness or lack of love.

Joe is now happily married. He ministers God's Word in a house church associated with the church where he was disciplined. Like the rest of us he is still subject to temptation. But unlike many of us he has learned a deeper integrity in his spirit and walk, observed by demons, men and angels. I found it hard not to weep for joy as I prayed with him.

12

The Return
of the
Prodigal

DR. ROBERT TYLER IS A RESEARCH physicist in Illinois, currently engaged in archaeological research. He is a warm, sensitive and engaging man, whose face lights up with compassionate truth. Though he has passed through deep waters, he has risen from them clean and whole.

He became a Christian at about the age of thirty. Before his conversion he practiced homosexuality, drank more than was wise and experimented with LSD. In a booklet he later wrote, he describes an LSD trip he underwent under experimental conditions. He affirms his conviction that drug use made him vulnerable to demonic malice.

At conversion he felt himself to be genuinely a new man in Christ and made immediate changes in lifestyle so as to live as a Christian should. But he did not for a long time realize the radical extent to which his entire life needed rebuilding from the ground floor up. Looking back now he realizes that Christians need more help at conversion. His church provided no assistance for the "pressing internal needs" he experienced at the time. "I was open to more help and cleansing . . . but gradually despaired as problems such as lust of the eyes and covetousness persisted. New converts need to come clean with a few of the trusted elders or leaders so that the new life begins on the strongest possible foundation."[1]

His search for inner healing was one motive in joining a local prayer group. He hoped it would be a forum in which "I could share my feelings of inadequacy, the low self-esteem I felt because of my past." But the prayer group lacked the depth necessary to give him the help he needed. "Though I had spent a fortune on psychoanalysis before becoming a Christian," he writes, "only rarely did I encounter the role of the New Testament priest as an intercessor or healing servant of God on my behalf. I believe that in-depth psychological counseling should be part of the church, not a separate function left for secular society to perform."

As I talked with Robert I sensed no bitterness when he referred to his earlier Christian experiences. He displayed no cynicism on reviewing his premature launching into public exposure and frantic pace of Christian service. Following his conversion, he preached widely, ran a Christian commune and was invited to speak at conferences and retreats. He played a reconciling role in the student riots and in the hippie movement. And he lived a celibate life.

The celibacy was not easy, and false accusations made his struggles harder. In the commune he welcomed men, some of whom were grappling with homosexual temptations. He deliberately and openly (though perhaps unwisely) displayed affection to everyone, and was accused falsely of having relapsed into gay practices.

A Father and a Son

By this time he had become involved in a growing Bible church which had a powerful ministry in the Chicago area and around the world. But the accusations had created a cloud of suspicion that refused to leave him. Lee Simpson, the most prominent among the church leaders, was troubled. Lee and the pastoral team met with Robert from time to time to pray with him and counsel him.

Even though there was not too great a disparity in their ages, Lee and Robert had an affectionate father-son relationship. Such, at any rate, is how Robert perceived the matter. He trusted and admired Lee as a father. Yet at the same time, he feared Lee as a powerful and authoritarian figure. Understandably, therefore, when Lee approached Robert about the suspicions and when Lee seemed uncertain about Robert's firm denial of homosexual practices, Robert was inwardly hurt and angry. He grew fearful of Lee and less certain about himself.

Robert's fear led to bitterness. Unaware of Lee's prayerful agony over the issue, Robert saw him only as a rejecting father. He began to feel there was little point in continuing to deny overt expression of his homosexual desires. "I don't know how to cope with this," he remembers thinking. He began to drink more heavily. At this point (while living in a permissive culture), homosexual temptation became easily rationalized. For years he had struggled against lustful fantasies. Now he fell into overt sexual sin with a younger man visiting from southern California. The young man's parents telephoned Lee who confronted Robert. Robert freely admitted his sin. But unhappily the telephone call reinforced Lee's suspicions that Robert had for some time been actively homosexual.

Lee and the rest of the church elders saw no alternative at that point but to announce Robert's failure to the church. The pastoral team had already spent time in prayer and counsel with him. As they saw it, Robert's continued presence in the church represented moral danger to younger men. As a final warning, Lee sent what Robert considered to be an angry letter demanding that he repent of *all* sin, which Robert took to refer to homosexual sins of which he had been falsely accused and including sins long ago which he had already confessed. The letter embittered and angered him. He felt misunderstood, humiliated, rejected. There was no way he could prove he had not been promiscuous all along. He was asked to resign his youth ministry immediately. He did so, but he also dropped out of the church, angry and disillusioned.

A dark period followed, and for the next five years Robert associated little with evangelical Christians. He publicly castigated the church and his former colleagues. He moved to a nearby community where he adopted two boys whose mother had committed suicide, boys with whom his relationship was wholesome and who constituted no homosexual temptation for him. But unforgiveness and bitterness froze his life. Humanly there seemed little hope of any spiritual restoration. In the months that followed he became an alcoholic, but miraculously stopped drinking completely though still away from God and the church.

But there came a day when Robert saw a vision of God in the glory of his holiness. With dismaying clarity he also saw his own sin and self-deception. The impact of the vision was overwhelming for him and temporarily he lost his reason and was hospitalized in a manic-psychotic state in which he remained for four days. A month of profound depression followed in which he knew he was in the hands of Satan and might die.

He repented. He got rid of the pornographic literature he had accumulated. He left the hospital by his own choice and continued to try to put everything in his life right. Uncertain whether he would live, he made a will. He joined a small church to regain a sense of fellowship with Christians, and for two years the tiny, godly congregation of Blacks and Asians ministered healing to him.

By now he realized that the business of his relationship with his former church had to be resolved. He was still unclear in his mind about the justice of the action of the pastoral team. But he was quite clear that his own bitterness toward Lee must be put aside. He might not have committed all the sins of which he felt he had been accused, but there had been other sins, among them such matters as pride and resentment.

After much prayer Robert wrote a general letter to Lee, asking that it be read to the entire church. In his letter he asked the members' pardon for betraying their trust in his spiritual leadership. He expressed a desire to meet with them. He knew he could not undo what he had done, but wished to do all he could to mend relationships. He offered to speak and pray with anyone who had any grievance against him.

Lee telephoned him at once, and the relationship which had been severed was restored. Robert was able to see how much he was cared for, and how deeply Lee and the others had mourned over him. A supper was arranged. While the pastoral team did not prepare a roasted calf, they did serve barbecued veal, and they presented him with a sports jacket and a gold ring, symbols of the return of the prodigal son. Robert was stunned and embarrassed by the warmth with which he was received.

Back among the general membership of the church, he found that the judgmentalism he had feared was clearly not there. He wondered if some of it had in fact been his own imagination. In any case his public confession had set him free from any fear of misunderstanding or rejection.

Lessons Learned

Many lessons can be learned from Robert's story. We already mentioned some of his own thoughts on his early Christian life. In a letter to Lee and the church elders, Robert later listed some ways to prevent tragedies like his own from occurring.

1. The Poor Start. There is substance to Robert's conviction that his Christian life got off to a bad start. His past was incompletely healed. He was exposed too precipitously to the stresses of Christian notoriety.

Training in holiness must include healing for the wounds of past sin and the sense of inferiority and unworthiness that gnaw at a Christian's faith. Strength is needed to cope with weaknesses which control the past. Too often we minister to these weaknesses with clichés and out-of-context Bible verses. The effects of a life of promiscuity and indulgence in alcohol are not automatically obliterated by Christian conversion. Christians may differ over how healing and strengthening could be brought about. But we must all agree that more time and trouble are needed, as well as deep sensitivity and discernment about an individual's needs.

Robert suggests, and we agree, that churches should provide, inside the Christian community, a Christian equivalent to secular psychotherapy. Some churches do. But tragically the model of counseling as well as its technique and philosophy sometimes remain worldly, even though biblical insights might be added. Christian counseling is professionalized, dividing the Christian public into the elite counselors and the psychological laity. The distinction should be one of degree and of gift, not merely of professional training, however valuable the training may be.

A turning to God on the part of the unconverted from socially unacceptable sins has begun in the West. It is possible that hundreds of thousands, if not millions of young men and women with every conceivable type of background, traumatized by abuse and every form of sin, will soon begin to be healed and made whole. Are there wise helpers to restore them, to give them a sound beginning in their Christian lives?

2. *The Dynamics of Church Relationships.* Psychoanalysts would be interested in Robert Tyler's "transference manifestations" toward Lee Simpson. *Transference* concerns the way we unconsciously misperceive someone because of unresolved conflicts from our childhood. Past experiences have placed scales on our eyes, scales which cause us to perceive others in a distorted fashion. Transference undoubtedly affected the way Robert viewed Lee. The state was set for his failure before he had even met Lee. Indeed the fact that Robert perceived Lee as a father whom he feared and yet whose approval he longed for, may have had little to do with Lee's actual attitudes and behavior toward him.

It was not harmful, however, for Robert to perceive Lee as a father. But it is important in such cases that both parties recognize what is happening and become more sensitive to any of their *hidden* neurotic needs. The father-son dimension to the relationship added to Robert's pain and difficulty. The same sort of complications arise frequently in church circles, and we could avoid pain and distress if we were more skilled in perceiving the distortions they can give rise to when we are not consciously aware of them.

3. *The Return of the Prodigal.* The barbecued veal, the eager

welcome and the gift of the sports jacket and the gold ring stand in startling contrast to the fear, suspicion and timidity with which most churches respond to repentant sinners. His reception astonished Robert and greatly helped his badly damaged self-identity. When I first heard of this incident I exploded with joy.

The measure of the pastoral team's generosity was the measure of their previous distress. The important thing is not that those who conduct corrective discipline never make a mistake, but that they share God's grief over those who wander far from him.

4. Divine Intervention. Jesus makes it clear in Matthew 18 that heaven backs corrective church discipline. Both case histories we have reported illustrate this. In Robert's case the vision of God's holiness proved to be the turning point. Without the discipline, that turning point might never have taken place.

God's dealings are mysterious. Was Robert right about the Satanic nature of his depression? We believe both the manic and the depressive episodes he describes to have been manifestations of the powers of darkness. We do not altogether know why they were permitted. We know from Nebuchadnezzar, Job and King Saul that Satanic afflictions may occur with divine permission. It is also clear from the Corinthian passage that the person expelled from Christian fellowship is exposed, for his or her soul's good, to the malice of Satan.

Certainly the effects were altogether good for Robert. Stripped of all illusions, even of the hope of life, he repented, made a will and systematically put all the wrongs in his life right. He turned around and began to walk a different path. We do wrong to deny needy church members the benefit of extreme church discipline.

5. Open Confession. Mean-spirited folk might say Robert did nothing in writing a letter to the general church membership, accusing him of merely telling the membership something they already knew. However, it is never a light matter freely to admit one's wrong. Moreover, the wrongs Robert confessed went beyond the wrongs of which he had been accused. He had become sensitive to issues like betrayal of trust, damage to the spiritual growth of others, bitterness, unforgiveness and self-deception. The confession manifested profound repentance.

And it did something nothing else could have done. Robert Tyler no longer cared who knew about his homosexual past. He no longer needed to be ashamed or to hide. He could look his fellow Christians in the eye, even those who might not understand him. He had become freed from the enslaving need to be approved of. Public confession of sin by a leader can have great value, not only to the church as a whole, but to the leader himself.

Earlier we said that church discipline frees. It would be truer of course to say that God frees and that God had shown Robert the road to freedom, a road he courageously chose to take. (Indeed his courage and freedom make the publication of this material possible, to the benefit of some who reading will experience a change in attitude.) Yet had the pastoral team not acted as they did, the freedom might never have resulted.

Robert Tyler is a man at peace with himself. To talk to him is to experience a kindling of divine joy. He constitutes a living and miraculous proof of the faithfulness of God, faithfulness to him personally and faithfulness to those who minister to him sacrificially in healing and in discipline.

13

Repentance

WHAT CONVINCED THE ELDERS IN JOE'S church that he was ready to be restored to fellowship? How did the pastoral board know that Robert Tyler also was ready? What is the place of confession in corrective church discipline? How grave does the sin have to be before we excommunicate sinners? What does one do when the pastor of a church or the head of a Christian organization is discovered to be living a Jekyll and Hyde existence? How does one deal with Christians who have a weakness for a particular sin (say drunkenness, drug addiction or a spirit excessively critical of fellow Christians) and who repent and then fall back repeatedly into sin?

In the chapters that follow we propose to deal with these and other practical issues. This chapter will be devoted to two questions: how can we discern true repentance? and, what role does our forgiveness play in corrective church discipline?

Asking the Right Questions

What degree of sin calls for excommunication? In the opening chapter we saw an example of a young woman who was dismissed from her church fellowship on the basis of the color of her car. Seventeenth-century Baptists in Britain might also excommunicate members who missed church services, played cards or kept "immodest company." But they would only do so after repeated admonition and when all hope of recovery was lost.[1]

In the other two illustrations in chapter one, alleged embezzlement of mission funds and an alleged affair were ignored. Does excommunication depend on the moral yardsticks and prejudices of different churches? Although it should not, in practice it usually does. But the original question (concerning the degree of sin calling for excommunication) is a question most commonly asked by people with no experience in corrective church discipline rather than by those who do.

Perhaps it is the wrong question. Perhaps we are too obsessed with the ax and too little with the head that will roll when it falls. If we hold to our original definition of church discipline (training in holiness of the church by the church), the approach to the problem at once begins to become clear. We cannot altogether ignore the gravity of a particular sin, yet with a different perspective we begin to focus more, as the seventeenth-century Baptists did, on a person's *resistance to reproof* than the gravity of a particular sin.

Does the sinner acknowledge sin? Is there a heart prepared to repent? Is there a willingness to change? An abhorrence of sin? Only sin that is not repented of, or else constitutes an ongoing moral danger in the flock, will call for extreme measures. So the question we should examine in this chapter is: What is true repentance and how can we recognize it?

The Nature of Repentance

Metanoia, the word most commonly translated "repentance" in the New Testament, is also translated "conversion." It implies an about-face, a radical change in direction. And as Donald Guthrie points out, Jesus preached a more radical repentance than the

Jewish teachers of his day.[2] To the Jews repentance meant a change in the face of the law, a behavioral change from disobeying it to keeping it. Jesus certainly called for changes, but they were to be changes arising from changed hearts, changed convictions, changed values—changes that would produce a totally new direction in life.

True repentance will always be a human response to something God does. Robert Tyler responded not only to the public announcement of his sin but to a vision of God's holiness, a vision followed by a totally changed view of himself, his life, his circumstances. At that point he set radical changes in motion. In the case of Joe, who had been crushed and despairing, it was a new and more vivid grasp the Holy Spirit gave him (through a book he read) of his relationship with Christ. Such was his joy that he could not refrain from showing it.

The two men were different. Their needs differed. Repentance in Robert was associated with depression and despair. In Joe it was finally made possible by joy. But both men responded *to something God was doing.* Their view of themselves and their lives was transformed. The behavior that followed resulted from the inner changes.

If we are not aware of God's initiative, or if we fail to expect it, we may never see the glory of transformed lives. Our expectations will be low. We may miss the glory of repentance in a sinner because we look at the sinner through the darkened lenses of our own unbelief. And this will be tragic. For we are called on to forgive those who repent. Repentance and forgiveness are linked in corrective church discipline (Lk 17:3-4), just as they are linked in the proclamation of the gospel (Lk 24:46-47). Our failure to perceive repentance when it is present will hinder the progress of the church.

Repentance does not *earn* forgiveness. Christ paid for our forgiveness by his death. But having paid the ransom he gave authority to forgive sins freely to us so that we now have authority to forgive others. We are called on to pronounce forgiveness to all who truly repent, who respond to the Word of God and to the Spirit of God.

History and Repentance

Unbelief may well have influenced the practice of church discipline. The business of the weepers, the hearers, the kneelers and the costanders described by Gregory the Wonder-Worker (which we mentioned in chapter one) and the eventual sentences of fifteen years of discipline for the sin of adultery, may have arisen because those who taught corrective discipline were looking at sin rather than at God. A rigid system leaves no room for God. Once you sentence an adulterer to fifteen years of discipline, you have already declared your conviction that the problem will not have been solved, and that true repentance will not have taken place before fifteen years have passed. If God is to work we must expect him to do so, and must make room for him to do so.

Could unbelief have been a major factor in the change of emphasis from repentance to *penitence* as the centuries rolled by? Penitence has to do with *our* making atonement, of our adding our prayers, our good works, our submission to a prescribed ritual of punishment, of alms-giving or going on a pilgrimage, to what Christ has already done. And the Western church from medieval times onward demanded penitence of church members who sinned, before she would forgive them.

Even from early times there was confusion on this issue. Tertullian, a very early Christian writer, was clear as to the meaning of *metanoia*.[3] Yet in one of his books he wrote, "How absurd it is to leave the penance unperformed, and yet expect forgiveness of sins! What is it but to fail to pay the price, and, nevertheless, to stretch out the hand for the benefit? The Lord has ordained that forgiveness is to be granted for this price: he wills that the remission of the penalty *is to be purchased for the payment which the penance makes.*"[4]

The idea of repentance had taken flight from Tertullian's understanding at that point, and penitence had taken its place. The work of the Spirit in stirring up repentance and the change of heart had been overlooked. And on a deeper level, the value of Christ's sacrifice was cheapened. It was now no longer enough to forgive sins.

Tertullian's view was not at first widespread. But during medieval times it gained ground steadily and finally replaced what Gustav Aulen calls the classic view of the atonement. Not until the Reformation did the older classic view (with its clearer understanding of repentance, and its dismissal of penance) emerge again.[5]

But our prime concern is not with historical origins but with reasons for the distortion of church discipline. If unbelief undermined the church's vision of the Holy Spirit's power to bring sinners to repentance and to transform lives, then unbelief can do so still. We shall not be able to perceive true repentance unless we believe it can take place. And if we cannot perceive it or believe in it, we may fall into the same errors about discipline that crippled or trapped our forefathers.

Discerning Repentance

Clearly then we must be prepared for God to work. Indeed if we have to make mistakes it would be better to mistake false repentance for true repentance than to shut out a truly repentant sinner. But discerning begins with looking. If we want to discern repentance, we must spend time talking with sinners. Sinners under discipline must be seen. Robert Tyler did not want to keep in touch with the pastoral team, so for seven years they had no means of knowing whether he was repentant. Once his letters had arrived, and there had been telephone and face-to-face conversations, Lee and his colleagues had no doubt that a work of God had taken place.

The elders who kept in touch with Joe were also sure, at least sure enough to reinstate Joe with temporary restrictions on his activities. Given, then, that we must expect to see God work, and must where possible expose ourselves to repentant sinners, by what criteria can we determine the genuineness of their repentance?

Obviously there must be change. In Robert's case the defiance and bitterness had ended. Of his own volition he had written to acknowledge his faults. More than this his attitude was clearly one of a man who had a changed view of himself and an increased sense of responsibility. Neither Joe nor Robert was trying to strike a bargain. Joe simply bore witness to a newfound joy. Robert expressed deep concern about the hurt he may have caused and was attempting to do anything he could to make restitution. He also took practical steps to shun temptation.

Most people who have to face repentant disciplinees do not acquire discernment overnight. Discernment is the daughter of experience and, sad to say, few people have much experience in talking to repentant sinners, even though many of us spend a lot of time counseling Christians with problems. Doctors and nurses often recoil from the stench and unpleasantness of cleaning pussy wounds. But personal distaste must be put aside out of compassion for the sufferer. So it is with sin. Experience can only be gained by dealing with it constantly. Yet God promises discernment. While experience will sharpen our discernment, the Holy Spirit can and will impart it if we are open to him. He is more concerned about repentant sinners than we are ourselves.

In addition charismatics talk about a "word of knowledge." Whatever the term we may use, it is clear from the New Testament that supernatural perception of a sinner's heart is also possible. Peter had no natural means of knowing that Ananias was attempting to con the church and to deceive God when he lay only a part of the proceeds of the sale of his property at the apostles' feet. Yet Peter's reaction was swift and devastating (Acts 5:1-11).

We must read the passage carefully however. Peter did not merely suffer from a vague feeling that something was wrong about Ananias' gift. He had a *precise knowledge* of his sin (deception in pretending to give all when he was under no compulsion to give any). And he announced the sin lucidly and unhesitatingly. Only someone who is tuned in to the voice of the Spirit can have so precise a knowledge. We must always be open to such a word from God, and be humble and honest enough not to pretend we have such supernatural insight when we don't.

How Many Times?

In the next chapter we shall look at those sins which continue to trick Christians however often they have repented of them, either in pretense or in sincerity. But before we do so we must look at the matter of forgiveness. We are to forgive those who repent *from the bottom of our hearts.* In doing so we shall minister Christ's forgiveness to them.

But what has *our* forgiveness to do with forgiveness of repentant disciplinees? Ought we not merely to pass on God's forgiveness, to administer forgiveness on heaven's behalf? It might appear so, but neither Scripture nor real life supports so simplistic a view.

Court judges and magistrates may strive to be impartial but cannot altogether prevent their personal feelings from influencing their judgment. No more can Christians who have to deal with repentant sinners. Whether we realize it or not, our discernment is subject to our personal attitudes. If we have pardoning and merciful dispositions, we will perceive matters differently from those who do not. We must look on people who have sinned without sentimentality, yet with a constant desire to forgive.

Our forgiveness is to be *personal.* That is, it must represent an accepting, loving attitude on our part which refuses to harbor resentment or remember the past. It is also an *authoritative* forgiveness. Heaven will agree with it (Mt 18:15-22).

Two things happen to us when we fail to be forgiving. We cease to be a channel of forgiveness, and we cease to experience the release of God's forgiveness toward us personally. Such is the lesson of Matthew 6:14-15 and 18:23-35. The second passage, of course, follows hard on the heels of the classic discipline passage. In it Jesus tells the story of the unforgiving servant whose enormous debt the king forgave. But later the king became enraged when he learned that the forgiven servant was persecuting one of his fellows for a petty sum. In his anger he flung the unforgiving servant in jail.

We are expected to have merciful and forgiving attitudes toward repentant sinners not because they deserve it, but *because God has been merciful and forgiving toward us.* We ourselves do not merit pardon. Moreover, forgiveness is something we can only keep when we give it away. Our capacity to perceive ourselves as forgiven shrivels to nothing when we refuse to forgive. We grow guilt-burdened and hard-hearted. An unhappy young single woman in one church had made an elder the target of her on-going resentment. Helen felt Michael had let her down in the hour of her deepest need by failing to support her. Several times Michael had met with her and had apologized and expressed his regret. Yet she clung to her unforgiveness.

Ken Blue met with the two of them. Helen stated her grievances again. After clarification and discussion Michael again asked for forgiveness for everything she had accused him of. The girl refused to receive his repentance and would not forgive because she believed he was not being sincere. They had arrived at the same impasse which had occurred several times before. When it became clear that Helen would not accept the elder's repentance, Ken explained that she was to forgive the elder fully or she would have to leave the church. She was shocked and began to cry. Seeing, however, that she had no choice she finally said she forgave the elder.

But as time passed the relationship between the two improved little. Ken decided subsequently that he probably had succumbed to impatience and had handled the matter badly. Forgiveness must come from a forgiving heart. Ken wondered if he himself had been impatient rather than forgiving. As for Helen, she may to this day be locked in a frozen pool of unforgiveness. She needs to know the melting warmth of God's forgiveness to her.

In the exercise of corrective church discipline, as in all our personal relationships, we will wind up either being channels of liberating pardon, or frightened and frozen pools. If we say we cannot forgive, or that though forgiving we cannot forget, we are really saying that we have never truly experienced the fullness of God's power toward us. It has failed to release those inner depths of our being. And in this case we have nothing to offer pardoned sinners except the sense of inner condemnation that still lurks somewhere deep within us.

Forgiveness must always be a joyful celebration. It is this that strikes such a warm chord in us as we read the "prodigal son" story of the church's welcome for Robert Tyler. Their response was heaven's own. There is more joy in the presence of the angels of God over a single repentant sinner than over a multitude of righteous persons who need no repentance (Lk 15).

But we may ask how realistic it is to pardon someone who *says* they have repented only to have him or her fall again and again. How realistic is Christ's answer to Peter, when the latter asked how many times he should forgive an offending brother? In the next chapter we will look more carefully at the kinds of sins that continue to haunt sinners.

14
Sins That Don't Go Away

SOME PEOPLE VIEW THE CHURCH AS AN army, others as a hospital. In favor of the hospital view is that earthly armies only accept perfect specimens. Military hospitals are therefore mainly for the wounded, or for those who managed to sneak in by hiding their imperfections.

The church on the other hand accepts imperfect specimens—sinners. Perfect specimens do not need Christ. Granted the church accepts redeemed, sanctified sinners. But they are sinners in whom the wounds from the Fall, plus in some cases the horrendous damage of their past environments and sinful habits, remain. So whether we are a hospital or an army, we are in the business of curing the sin sick and the sin wounded.

In this chapter we shall focus on long-term sins, what some people call *besetting* sins, specific sins arising from specific weaknesses. The word is borrowed from Hebrews 12:1 in the King

James Version, ". . . the sin which doth so easily beset us . . ."
Whatever the writer may have meant by the phrase, it has come
to symbolize what we might call *addictive sins,* like alcohol abuse,
a bad-tempered disposition, perpetual grouchiness, a critical spirit,
habitual gossip, pornography addiction. All of us have specific
weaknesses to specific failings, but some of these are more
troublesome than others.

We do not need Joe's story to convince us. Whatever our theological position on sanctification may be, we are forced to admit
from observation of the church scene that besetting sins are still
with us. Many of us never seem to outgrow our weaknesses. And
besetting sins are divided (as we have pointed out) into socially
acceptable sins (like pride and gossip) and socially unacceptable
sins (like alcohol abuse and drug addiction).

But the quality common to both is that they keep on happening.
That is, Mary continues to have temper tantrums, Bill continues
to get drunk from time to time, and Suzanne is into her fifth affair,
even though each seemed to have repented, claimed victory, been
resanctified (if such a thing is possible) or whatever. And it is the
repetitiveness that throws us. We begin to avoid such people. We
form rejecting attitudes toward them, placing them in a class apart
from the rest of us who can at least manage to keep up appearances.

Christian churches are haunted by unhappy Christians who
don't "have victory" over specific sins. We have suggested remedies, but by and large they have made little permanent impact.
Within our ranks are the ongoing angry, bitter, untruthful,
alcoholic, drug addicted, porn addicted, promiscuous, greedy,
gossips and so on.

In the case of socially unacceptable besetting sins, sinners
preserve their secrets for as long as they can. Frequently we aid
and abet them in this because we too prefer not to know. We don't
want to be bothered with the embarrassment and the general
mess. We don't want to be burdened with the sinners' unending
struggles. But they and their secrets are with us.

Why does this situation exist? What is the reason for the sort
of church schizophrenia in which we believe (or else pretend we

believe) that all is well apart from a few unmentionable people, when all the time our ranks are infiltrated by the defeated and the impotent, grappling hopelessly with their besetting sins. They are our wounded brothers and sisters. They are the church's closet pariahs.

There are many reasons for the schizophrenia, but four stand out: Christian naiveté, Christian worldliness, Christian selfishness and churches that are not churches, churches that have ceased to function as they claim to. And we shall have to spend some time dealing with these before we discuss the sins themselves.

Christian Naiveté and Christian Worldliness

We are naive about sin, about indwelling sin. So impressed are we by the potential of the victorious Christian life (a potential that cannot be exaggerated) that we have underestimated sin's power and the malice of the Satanic hordes under whose shadows we live. We have even forgotten simple things like the power of long-standing habits. We are so victory-conscious that we have ceased to fear sin. Our doctrinal beliefs cannot be squared with the defeated strugglers in our midst. We feel they ought not to be there so we refuse to see them.

But we are not merely naive about sin; we are blind to it. And as churches we have become so because we are worldly. We once thought of worldliness as a matter of smoking, drinking, dancing, jewelry, cosmetics, movies—and even in these ways we are becoming "worldly." Yet these things do not constitute worldliness. At worst they are only symptoms of worldliness. They might or might not be symptomatic of the underlying disease, but they are not the disease itself. Worldliness goes deeper than painted lips or silver screens.

Biblical worldliness is described by the apostle John, who tells us, "Do not love the world or the things in the world. If any one loves the world, love for the Father is not in him" (1 Jn 2:15). To what world does John refer? Clearly in the sense of the age, the age we live in with its values and goals. What then are the "things in the world" we are to eschew? "For all that is in the world, the lust of the flesh and the lust of the eyes and the pride of life, is not of the Father but is of the world" (1 Jn 2:16). Is the apostle oversimplifying things? Can our age be summarized so succinctly? Indeed it can. Worldliness is not a list of do's and don'ts. Its essence lies in three lusts—of the flesh, of the eye and of pride. It is an attitude of heart. To be worldly is to have one's heart-love stolen away from the Father and replaced by lusts.

There is the lust of the flesh, by which John may refer to legitimate bodily appetites (for food, sleep, sex and so on). These become lusts when we raise them to the level of demigods before whom we bow and for whom we live. In that case lusts are legitimate appetites to which we have become slaves. Or else John could be using "flesh" in the Pauline sense of the term, referring to carnal lusts, the worship not merely of normal bodily appetites, but sinful appetites as well.

The lust of the eye is the worship of beautiful things, the desire and the will to possess them. There is nothing wrong with beauty. There is nothing wrong with wanting something beautiful. The question is: How much is it wanted? More than we want the Father's will? What price are we prepared to pay to get what we want?

As for the pride of life, the pride against which all of us struggle, it requires no explanation. It needs only conviction and repentance.

Can worldliness be reduced to three simple principles? John seems to think so. Let us adopt another expression for lust—*the pursuit of pleasure,* the pursuit of bodily pleasure, the pursuit of possessions that give us pleasure and the pursuit of excessive self-esteem and respect of others that give us pleasure. To pursue these things is to be what is known as a hedonist. And what we are saying is that Christian churches have been desensitized to sin by hedonism. Let us be very clear about the matter. There is nothing wrong with pleasure. All the devil can do is teach us how to abuse it.

We have, however, been brainwashed into believing that certain things are *necessary* for us. We are bombarded by the values that control the world around us. They drench our brains by a jet of verbiage from the media, from films and from our educational system. Values are assumed in almost every conversation we engage in, in every discussion we overhear. Slowly, without any argument, the sheer volume and weight of the world's opinions have obliterated a more heavenly view.

"Give yourself a break. *You deserve it,*" says the commercial. "I'm worth every penny of it," asserts the film star about his outrageous earnings. We have heard of a charter of rights that talks about our *right* to five freedoms and as Christians we accept unquestioningly our right to many more. The atmosphere we breathe is an atmosphere that assumes such rights. And with the rise of the human potential movement, the right to our total fulfillment as human beings has now been added.

We assume our right to sexual fulfillment, our right to satisfy our many emotional "needs." Was Jesus sexually fulfilled? Was Paul? Did they need to be to fulfill their goals? Do we?

Once we call something a right, we begin to assume that it is more important than it actually is. Life is more than food and drink and possessions. There are more important things in life than sex and self-esteem here and now. For we are at war with principalities and powers. And from time to time war calls for sacrifice, pain, suffering and bone weariness.

In our worldliness we have lost a sense of perspective and have adopted the perspective of the age we live in. So to the ambitious we offer worldly distinction, to the philanderer sexual fulfillment and to the alcoholic freedom to enjoy a glass of wine. We do so unintentionally, but we do so nonetheless, and we do so because the world has slowly brainwashed us, corroded our standards, distorted our perspective.

We say we are rich and need nothing. We do not know that we are pitiable, blind and naked. And in our blindness we do not see sin around or within our ranks as it really is. Blindness protects us. We are called on, however, to repent, to buy eternity-gold, be clothed in white raiment and to purchase eye ointment to cure our blindness.

Christian Selfishness
Another reason the church is ineffective in dealing with besetting

sins is because we are confused about our roles in the church and about our priorities. It takes time to help someone with a besetting sin. And time is money, even to Christians. The common feeling among Christians is either that looking after such things is the pastor's job, or that if the pastor doesn't have time, then we should hire a professionally trained Christian counselor to look after them. In this way the rest of us can remain free to get on with the business of living.

Ken Blue and I do not question the value of Christian counseling, provided that it is both competent and truly Christian. We are fortunate that God in his sovereignty has given us both specific and general revelation. He has given us scientific insights as part of natural revelation, and we must be good stewards of the knowledge that we have. But we ought not to be saddling Christian counselors with problems that we as the church should be dealing with as part of church discipline (both in the broad and in the corrective senses of the term).

Sinners who struggle need acceptance, understanding, encouragement and admonition *from the body of Christ*. The reason we are so helpless in the face of their problems is not that we lack training, but because we are unwilling to put in the time and because we are afraid. We are unwilling to make ourselves vulnerable in group sharing and prayer. And our unwillingness is in part due to the fact that a myriad of activities and committees in the church, however worthwhile, are already taking up all our time.

Many of us belong to churches that are more like Christian clubs than real churches. Like clubs they are administered by a professionally trained, salaried staff. Volunteers from among the general membership fill committees and run regular activities. We have not paused to ask what our real needs and goals are. We are too busy trying to keep what we have running as smoothly as possible. Club-type churches have nothing to offer people with besetting sins.

I had what some people would call a "dirty old man" referred to me recently. But he was a Christian educator with seminary training. He had been picked up by the police for sexually fondling little girls. The police and the pastor of the man's church felt that a psychiatrist, preferably a Christian psychiatrist, should handle the matter. But it quickly became evident to me that the man's real needs were to be understood with acceptance, to repent of his sin and to have firm but kindly limits imposed by those closest to him.

He had no insight into his weakness. He thought perhaps he should have a ministry in the Sunday school, perhaps with a class of little girls. He also lacked any real sense of the destructiveness of his actions in young lives. Prolonged counseling or psychotherapy (both with the man and with his wife) might or might not have produced the insight he so badly needed. But insight could also have been produced by a community that understood him, accepted the fact that he had a weakness, and leveled with him both about its seriousness and about the relationship between weakness and sin.

As part of corrective church discipline it should have been made clear to him that under no circumstances was he to have contact with little girls, since this represented temptation for him. Christians are to flee temptation.

He also needed a Christian friend who could pray with him regularly, possibly a Christian couple who could do the same with the man and his wife. His behavior needed to be monitored, but with understanding and loving acceptance. Eventually he might have needed the full force of corrective discipline to help him see the horror of his sin and the grace of a loving God.

We began this section by saying that it takes time to help someone with weaknesses of this sort. It also takes tolerance, not of the sin, but of the sinner. Yet we shrink back discomfited, embarrassed. Into our heads pop words like *weirdo, strange*. He is some kind of disagreeable curiosity, the kind we would rather avoid. After all, what do you say to a "dirty old man"? We are horrified, disgusted. Is one supposed to love such a creature?

Yes. Our sins might be different, but to God they are no less reprehensible. Like him we are nothing more than redeemed sinners. We deserve God's grace not one atom more than he does. He is our brother. A pathetic brother perhaps, but a hungry human being who needs an environment of love, honesty and firmness. Churches should be that environment. But they are not.

The Harm of Besetting Sins

All sins are harmful, but habitual sins are harmful in two distinct ways. There is what we might term *primary* damage and *secondary* damage. Primary damage is to the sinners and to anyone else their sins affect. Secondary damage is to the sinner's own inner being and his or her capacity to relate to God.

A perpetual drunkard damages his body, ruins his chance of a happy family life and often ruins his career. In the process he can create havoc for others, especially those nearest him, his family and friends. If the drunkard is a woman, she can damage her unborn child. Some drunkards beat their spouses and create hatred and fear in their children. Others kill people in traffic accidents, bringing grief and pain to other families. These are all examples of primary damage.

In the case of the Christian who was double-billing his clients (p. 33), the primary damage was to the people he robbed. In the case of people with critical spirits, they damage the lives of those they unnecessarily castigate and disrupt the unity of the body generally. There may be obvious primary damage in the case of a man addicted to pornography if his wife runs across his literature. In that case she may be hurt and humiliated. But often she will be aware that her relationship with her husband is not the same.

Secondary damage is to the sinner's inner being, to his or her relationship with God. How do you cope if you go on doing things you know to be wrong? You have to live with yourself. Conscience becomes unbearable, so you gag it. You begin to lie to yourself, to make excuses and, in the case of socially unacceptable sins, you learn to lie to others as well. Inward corruption reigns. Worse than gagged, your conscience becomes seared and scarred.

Alcoholics sneak drinks, lie about their drinking, may hide their bottles and do a good cover-up job. Wife beaters present a normal smiling front. Pornography buffs hide their magazines in drawers and under mattresses. But to live a double life is soul destroying.

Inner dishonesty is spiritually crippling. It is not merely that you learn to lie, but that you learn to lie to yourself, and to have an imaginary relationship with God. Primary damage is damage in time. Spiritual damage is damage in eternity, that is, damage that may put you in the category of those who will be saved, "yet so as by fire."

The real problem in church discipline is less the primary damage than the inner corruption that inevitably flows from habitual sin. It is hard for most of us to be honest with ourselves all the time, but for people who are in the grip of habitual sin the deepest damage is the evergrowing tendency to deceive themselves. Spiritual self-deception may be the hardest nut to crack in the practice of corrective church discipline.

The Church and the Alcohol Abuser

It is impossible in a book of this size to enter into a detailed discussion of the many kinds of habitual sins in which Christians become trapped. We have already mentioned lying, gossip, pornography addiction, habitual alcohol and drug abuse, idleness, sexual promiscuity, child molestation, homosexuality, child abuse (or battering) and wife beating. We could add to the list. The fact that they are not only sinful but that they seem to be impossible to shake raises the question of how responsible the sinners are. Do we view them as sinners needing corrective church discipline, as sick people needing a cure or as both? Are demons involved? Is there a place for professional help, and if so what is it?

To answer these questions let us take one example of a besetting sin which reflects features characteristic of most if not all of the sins in the list. Let us look at the case of alcohol abusers. And by alcohol abusers we do not only refer to people who wind up in the gutter, but simply those who drink more than they should.

But should Christians drink alcohol at all? We feel that there should be freedom of conscience in the matter. Scripture nowhere condemns drinking, but does condemn drunkenness. In addition the book of Proverbs gives severe warnings about how treacherous alcohol can prove. It is likewise our observation that alcohol is currently much more of a curse than a blessing in society. In view of society's increasing problems with alcohol, churches should give serious thought to instructing and warning church members about the danger of alcohol abuse and Christian responsibility to avoid causing others to stumble.

But they must have clear reasons for any policies they adopt, and make their reasons plain to young people and to new members. Most churches that condemn drinking give no explanation of their prohibition. They merely indicate that to drink is a sin or else give invalid or untrue reasons for abstention.

What about those who drink too much? Their situation has the following features:

1. We have been taught to think of alcoholism as something to be treated by experts. (The same is true of homosexuality, temper outbursts, habitual lying and others.)

2. We tend to form rejecting attitudes to alcohol abusers. The worse they get, the more we avoid them, as we do in the case of other sinners.

3. Alcohol abusers learn to deceive themselves and others. They refuse to believe they have a problem. They live double lives.

4. Their consciences become corrupt.

5. They seem unable to comprehend the harm they do to others, or if they do see it, to accept responsibility for it.

6. They are helplessly gripped by their habit and will remain so as long as they deny this to themselves.

There is widespread controversy among experts and would-be experts about whether alcohol abuse is an illness, about what causes it and about how to treat it. The fact that there is such widespread disagreement among experts is an indication that no ideal solution has yet been found. Nevertheless, we believe that if churches functioned as they ought to function, and if church discipline were what it ought to be, then many closet alcohol abusers could be helped more by their own church than by any other agency.

But is alcoholism a sin or is it a sickness? The problem with referring to behavior as _sick_ is that we view the word as being incompatible with _bad._ We sympathize with sick people but hold bad people responsible for their actions.

Talcott Parsons was a sociologist who studied sickness as a social phenomenon. He popularized the terms *the sick role* and *the medical model*. He saw sickness as a drama—relatives, friends and doctors all playing a role around the principal actor who has the sick role. Parsons was not saying that sickness did not exist. Like the rest of us he believed in cancer. What interested him was the changed behavior, the shifts in attitude and responsibility that took place around the sick person. If dad is not lazy but dying of cancer, we suddenly stop blaming him. We are overcome with guilt. We put him to bed, feed him and show him deep concern. Friends bring him flowers or send him cards. We summon the doctor and await his pronouncements (and his bill) with fear and trembling.

Many people have not really grasped what Parsons was saying. The fact that we were wrong to blame dad for laziness does not necessarily mean dad no longer has responsibility for anything in life. It does not mean he now can do no wrong. Yet the word *sick* when applied to things like alcoholism, lying, gossiping or general crankiness, automatically induces this kind of switch in our thinking.

A shift in attitude may be necessary, but it should perhaps be a little less extreme. People with besetting sins are in real difficulty and need help. But *vulnerability* to sin does not excuse it. Even if the vulnerability to alcohol addiction is inherited,[1] addicts must still accept responsibility for their lives.

The fact that alcohol abusers may be born with a vulnerability to alcohol also means that they are no different from the rest of us. All of us are born with specific vulnerabilities, weaknesses to specific forms of sin. Potential alcoholics have a weakness toward a sin which differs from our own weaknesses only in how destructive it is of their own and other people's well-being. They live with a time bomb inside them, a time bomb that starts to tick the moment they begin to drink.

If churches have a message worth listening to, then it is a message addressed to repentant sinners who are in bondage to sin. Yet we cannot be simplistic about the gospel. It has incomparable power to deliver. But it must be rightly apprehended and applied.

Lessons from Alcoholics Anonymous

Alcoholics Anonymous (usually called A.A.) claims to have a better cure rate than any other organization or group. The claim is probably just. The expertise of its members is impressive. Yet A.A. views alcoholism as a sickness, not as a sin. We must ask what we can learn from them and why, having a faulty philosophy, they can do so much, when most churches, having so much, do so little. Let's consider five points.

First, A.A. alleviates guilt. The alcoholic is told that alcoholism is a sickness. Remember Talcott Parsons and the sick role. When the word *sick* penetrates an alcoholic's mind, a change in his perspective takes place. You can't do anything about sickness. You need help. Your problem will call for a different lifestyle and a new philosophy. Alcohol is killing you, and you won't ever be able to touch it again. But it's not your fault that you're an alcoholic. Thus guilt is alleviated and hope is born.

The gospel expresses the matter in more accurate and more powerful terms, if it is preached properly. "He breaks the power of canceled sin . . ." Does he? We should know. But do we? In how many churches is guilt being canceled, repentance manifested and the chains of sin broken every week? Churches have an answer to alcoholic guilt. Yet alcoholics show no interest. By and large they avoid churches because churches are not equipped to give help. So sinners plagued by besetting sin cry out for the relief of a pardoning and accepting God. To be freed from guilt is the first step on their road to freedom from sin itself. God has freedom in abundance to offer, freedom from guilt.

Second, A.A. forces alcohol abusers to face their helplessness. Again, the church is as woefully inadequate in this as it is in relieving guilt. Alcoholics have to admit that their lives are out of control and that they cannot manage them. Only when a sinner with besetting sin recognizes this same fact at a deep level is there hope. Corrective church discipline may be needed to achieve this. God's power is not unleashed so long as sinners cling to hope in their own resources. True hope can only rise from the dust of despair.

When sinners tell us they are in despair, we must have compassion. But we must ask them whether they are telling the truth. Do they really recognize the hopelessness of their condition, or are they feeling sorry for themselves? Joe in chapter eleven had to discover how deep was the pit he was trapped in before he could understand the power of Christ.

Third, A.A. forces alcohol abusers to face their internal dishonesty. Its members have great expertise in unmasking the inner deceits of alcohol abusers. They have experience and (as we shall discuss in a moment) they know their own hearts. While sin is not called sin, A.A. encourages its members to deal with sin by having them make "a fearless moral inventory." They review their past and admit the wrongs they have done to others. They take a good look at themselves, are encouraged to apologize to others and make wrongs right. Subsequently, they may go over the list of such wrongs with their sponsor, an older or more experienced A.A. member.

Do churches encourage members to search their hearts? A.A. members confess their faults to one another, occasionally with, though more usually without, prayer. Christians pray but don't confess to one another. What would happen in churches if we were to divide up in pairs once a month (or even once a year) for Fearless Moral Inventory Sunday?

Fourth, A.A. provides a detailed plan, twelve steps on the roadway to freedom. Each step is clearly described. Plus each person is assigned a guide or mentor in the form of a sponsor. Some churches are beginning to take detailed training of young disciples seriously, but more, much more can be done.

Lastly, A.A. provides a supportive, nonjudgmental, caring community where many alcoholics feel at home and at ease. This does not mean that their fellow members do not level with them. No punches are pulled in A.A. But A.A. members tend to be less conscious of their moral superiority than Christians. They have more of a "neither do I condemn thee" attitude.

There are, of course, drawbacks to A.A. Most Christians are

critical of the defective theology in the movement, which arose from the same spiritual roots as Moral Re-Armament. But so long as churches remain powerless to help alcoholics, their criticisms, while being accurate, will sound hollow. It is a sad indictment of local churches that we should have to recommend they send people with alcohol problems to their local A.A. After all, has A.A. not imitated what rightfully belongs to Christianity while we have given up our birthright in these areas?

We began the chapter by asserting that we fail to deal with besetting sins because we are naive, worldly, selfish and because we no longer function as true churches.

We would rapidly lose our naiveté if we were to get involved with sinners, whether those sinners be alcoholics, pornography addicts or perpetual gossips. Worldliness and selfishness call for repentance. And we shall function as true churches when we reintroduce church discipline.

Special Counselors

Special counselors (we say *special* counselor because just as we are all priests, so we must all be counselors) may be of help in two or three areas. They may have a firmer grasp of biblical principles. Or they may have skills in facilitating communication among family members where this (as in the case of alcohol abuse) is clearly needed. They may have extra knowledge of one particular form of besetting sin. Professional counselors must beware, however, of isolating those who consult them from the fellowship of the church or of having clients look to the counselor as a substitute for regular Christian fellowship.

Again, while it may be true that most sins that grip people are not illnesses in the normal sense of the term, they may arise out of such illnesses occasionally. I discuss this in considerable detail in *The Masks of Melancholy*,[2] explaining how disturbed brain biochemistry may, in addition to the particular form of emotional disturbance it gives rise to, also be associated with sexual aberrations and promiscuity, blasphemous obsessions, excessive drinking, outbursts of murderous rage and many other sinful thoughts and actions. Once the brain physiology is normalized those tendencies will either disappear altogether, or become infinitely easier to control. The illnesses are much commoner than we once suspected.

Clearly special counselors should be trained in the early recognition of such illnesses (a training often inadequate in many courses in Christian counseling) so that sufferers may be treated by a physician. Counselors, like Christians in general, must also have some understanding of occult phenomena, and be able to perceive and deal with the demonic.

If the church is a hospital, it functions with woeful inadequacy. Our sin-sick members hide from us in shame. They know we cannot help them unless we change radically. Yet we could help them if we were really about our Master's business instead of playing at church. Let no one suppose that the serious business of dealing with sin of this sort is easy. It is hard and costly. And the changes that must come about among us, both spiritually and structurally, are many and difficult. We shall continue to look at them in subsequent chapters.

15

Confessing Sin

"CONFESS YOUR SINS TO ONE ANOTHER, and pray for one another, that you may be healed" (Jas 5:16).

At some point church discipline (especially in its broader, training aspects) has to concern itself with confession of sin. Could James have guessed the wild excesses or the heated controversies his gentle words would lead to? Few of us are comfortable with the idea of confession. Confess? How much? To whom? Under what circumstances?

Confession in Secret
Roman Catholics often think of confession as something you go to—at least once a year, say, at Christmas or Easter. Protestants prefer not to think about it at all. Moral Re-Armament on the other hand perceives it as a sort of ethical group sauna from which you emerge cleansed and invigorated, having sweated your

filth out. Most of us prefer discretion when it comes to bean spilling. Isn't there something unhealthy about focusing on personal sin, especially in public? ". . . whatever is pure, whatever is lovely, whatever is gracious . . ." (Phil 4:8). Not scandal! If we are given the privilege of going to God's very throne, and in secret, should not this be enough? "No," James stubbornly insists, "Confess your sins to one another."

Confession has odd psychological aspects to it. For instance, it is sometimes easier to confess a sin to God than to one's neighbor. And though it would be nice to account for the difference by saying that God is kind and understanding whereas our neighbor might not be, honesty compels us to admit that the explanation fails to get to the root of the matter.

Another curious aspect of confession is that confessing a sin to a friend can give me the kind of relief that confessing to God does not. My friend and my neighbor are "real." My confession to them represents a real transaction to me. Can it be that my confession to God has ceased to be real?

God is real. His reality is not in question. Rather, we have learned how to insulate ourselves from his heat—to wall him off psychologically. He has ceased to be a real person to us, at least in the area of sin.

There are two ways in which this can happen. Some people are so conscience stricken, so tuned in to the terrible denunciations of Satan the Accuser, that they cannot believe that God either hears or forgives them. Such people are insulated from the warmth of his grace. They drag their weary feet through an icy sludge of guilt because they have walled themselves off from his hot winds of grace.

Some of us have misunderstood the doctrine of grace. We have supposed that since Christ died for us, God no longer recoils in loathing from our sinful actions. God forgives. He loves. We are his children. The death of his Son atones for us. Why then should God loathe our sinful actions? *We have forgotten that Calvary has made no difference to God's attitude to sin.* He cannot bear to look on it. That which cost him the death of his Holy One remains and ever will remain of utmost abhorrence to him.

We have subtly distanced ourselves from this aspect of his nature. We treat him with unconscious contempt. It would bother us to shock or grieve a friend. But God's grief and shock no longer affect us. We do not feel them. We say we reverence him and we believe what we say, but we do not even respect him. We would experience more relief from getting matters straightened out with an angry garbage collector than with an angry God. Our understanding of God's grace has become devalued to what Bonhoeffer derides as "cheap grace."

Here then is the rule: If it fills you with deep shame to confess to a close friend what is easily confessed to God, then your confession to God is in some sense unreal. The shame validates the transaction. Confession is not merely a verbal description of thoughts and actions. People who truly confess to God no longer care whether others learn their secret. The relief that floods them is such that it flushes away their shame as well as their guilt.

The practice of confessing our faults to another human being can in fact make the Godward transaction more real. Confession is meant (among other things) to heal. James's exhortation ends with the words, ". . . and pray for one another, that you may be healed." Physical and emotional disease can arise from unresolved sin. Confession is meant to involve a real encounter with a real person. It is intended to produce healing. If the encounter with a fellow human can help the divine encounter become more real to us, then we had better take a serious look at the practice of confession.

There are of course problems. History presents us with many models of confession, and we shall have to ask which are the more biblical. How public, for instance, should the confession of our private sins be? Origen agreed with the early fathers that confession of sin should be made public. Private sins might well be confessed in private first, but once confessed in private they were to be publicly confessed.

Few of us would agree with Origen and the early fathers (though there are church groups who do). If he wanted to encourage confession, even private confession, he was going about it in an odd way. Most people would think twice about confessing sins to Origen if they knew beforehand that a public ordeal would follow.

Over the centuries the issue became a critical one. In the course of time the conviction grew that what you confessed (especially to a priest) should not be broadcast, but kept absolutely secret. People began to speak of the *seal* of confession. The confessor sealed the priest's lips. And to this day in several countries, while psychiatrists can be held in contempt of court for not answering damaging questions about their patients, priests enjoy legal immunity.

If we continue to deal with the matter of confession on a practical plane we can see at once that a sinner is more likely to reveal his sin to someone with whom his secret is absolutely safe. If you want to get adultery off your conscience, then go to a priest you can trust. But on a spiritual plane we have to ask what confession is all about. If (as we were arguing a few paragraphs back) one of the objects of confessing our sins to someone else is that a more real transaction, an interpersonal transaction, may take place, does not secrecy defeat this purpose? So long as private confession to God remains secret, there is a danger of it becoming unreal as we "psychologically distance" God, and make confession a phony and meaningless procedure. Is not the same danger present in *all* secret confession?

One of my Roman Catholic patients who recently has entered into a glorious understanding of the work of Christ told me of a visit she had just made to her priest for confession. "Shall we go into the confessional booth or shall we speak face to face out here?" he asked. She was startled. To look at him and confess seemed far more threatening than to speak to him from her side of the confessional booth.

Secret confession to a priest was part of an act of repentance by which absolution was granted to the repentant sinner. The priest (and this was one reason the Reformers reacted so strongly to the system) stood in the place of God. Secret confession to the priest was in fact secret confession to God. Thus while unrepentant Catholics may go through a meaningless ritual in confessing to a priest, Protestants can do the same before God's throne.

Unfruitful Confession

One purpose of confession that we have already touched on is that we may be healed, healed from the pathological consequences of unresolved sin, whether these be physical, emotional, social or spiritual. Therefore one criterion by which we can determine the form of the confession will be whether that form contributes to healing. Is it restorative? And if we see confession as part of the church's training in holiness, we shall ask, "Does the form of the confession enhance reconciliation, purify and edify the church, promoting spiritual liberty?"

Confession can be a form of exhibitionism, in secret as well as in public. I recently received a letter from a young man I had never met accompanied by his photograph. The letter began with an appeal for me to help him by giving him counsel on sins he had not dared to confess to his counselor. In the letter he described explicit details of his sexual sins and feelings. As I read, I became painfully aware that he was indulging in a subtle form of seductive exhibitionism. His private confession benefited neither of us. It was both narcissistic, exhibitionistic and constituted an invitation for me to play the voyeur.

Another type of unfruitful confession is sometimes heard at A.A. meetings. Some members rise at meetings only to indulge in a sort of competition, the winner being the member who can tell the most horrendous story of past sins and failures. Such confessions are made in an attempt to awaken admiration. They are shameless. They restore nobody. They edify nobody, not even the person making the confession.

Yet confession can heal. Perhaps confession is most dramatically therapeutic when the person making the confession no longer cares who knows about his or her sin, so great is the burden of concealment. Both Ken Blue and I have been present in church services where, as the Holy Spirit dealt with them, scores of men and women spontaneously and publicly cried out their broken confessions of sin, not caring who around them heard. Too many were weeping brokenly for anyone to watch with dry eyes. And as Christians moved in to minister God's Word and to pray, the darkness on pain-filled faces gave place to a peaceful shining.

One issue at the time of the Reformation was how much should be confessed. Catholic doctrine had since Innocent III insisted that every sin, however small, must be confessed at least once a year if it were to be forgiven. Such a rule might present no problem to people with relaxed consciences, but to the meticulous and the scrupulous the system was a nightmare. Both Lutheran and Reformed traditions firmly rejected it. Confession was not a coin to buy pardon with.

As McNeill points out, "the meticulous enumeration of detailed sins may set up an obsession and prove a hindrance to deliverance."[1] So in 1520 Martin Luther in his book *Confitendi Ratio* rejected the demand of Innocent III for total confession, pointing out that it was an impossible one. (Can you remember all your own sins during the past seven days? The sins not only of commission but omission? Those of deed and word and thought? Those of subtle motivation?) Had we all the most perfect memories in the world, and the most exact knowledge of ethics, we would, if such a demand were of God, spend much of our time committing sin and the rest of it trying to think out what needed to be confessed. The evil of the system lies in its power to paralyze men and women, and to grind them into the ground with a sense of hopeless guilt.

Calvin likewise would have none of it. ". . . it follows that . . . those who use [confession] according to their need [should] neither be forced by any rule, nor be induced by any trick to recount all their sins. But let them do this so far as they consider it expedient, that they may receive the perfect fruit of consolation."[2]

When Confession Is Good

Calvin rejected the idea that confession should be an enforced rule. But what principle should guide us as we train our fellow believers in holiness? No single principle can in isolation be a criterion. We should judiciously blend some of the following:

Confession is good *when it opens the way to deliverance and healing for the sinner*. The teaching of James affirms the relationship between healing and confession. Many writers agree about the relationship between the resolution of sinful bondage (sometimes by confession) and physical and emotional health.

Confession is good *when it startles us into a deeper awareness of the sinfulness of sin.* The Roman Catholic woman I mentioned earlier became startlingly aware of this when her priest suggested she make her confession outside the booth.

Confession is good *when it benefits the person or persons who hear the confession.* At times a public confession may serve to encourage and hearten the whole congregation, especially where the confession focuses on God's gracious pardon and deliverance. What otherwise would be an invitation to voyeurism can become a message of release and forgiveness. "So *he* [or she] had the problem too! I'm so glad I'm not alone. And it's obvious that God delivered. . . ." Confession is bad when it is self-centered, stage grabbing or designed to impress.

Confession is good *when a Christian leader has been deceiving or sinning against those who are led.* A public confession can never be forced. Yet under these circumstances public confession can be wholesome both to leader and led. It can prepare the way for a later resumption of leadership by giving the sinning leader freedom from having to hide. But this can only occur when the confession flows from a deeply repentant heart.

Clearly there is no point in the confession being made to a wider public than to the people immediately affected by the sin. Even so it may dismay those who have been betrayed. But it can have the benefit both of forcing them to see that leaders are exposed to great pressure and temptation, and (if the leader's repentance is real) it can move them to deeper devotion and prayer as they view the leader's brokenness before a holy God and contemplate the tragedy of sin. As we said in an earlier chapter, however, sexual sins of church members which do not in any way involve a wider public should not be confessed publicly.

Confessing our sins to others can be filled with rich benefits and fraught by serious perils. To use common parlance, it is a "high-risk, big-payoff deal." Those whose motives in confession are pure and who confess under appropriate circumstances may reap for themselves and give to others a harvest of blessing. Those who confess carelessly and in secret may reap only hardness of heart. Those who confess wrongly also damage their own souls, and in addition may wound and cause to stumble all who listen to them.

16
When Leaders Go Wrong

JAMES J. MACDONELL, FORMER AUDITOR general of Canada, was once quoted in the Toronto *Globe and Mail* as saying, "Accountability is the price exacted for the gift of power." Accountability— the price of power? Macdonell was thinking of secular political power. Do his words apply to Christian leaders?

Political power flourishes among Christian churches and organizations. Sometimes it is used kindly and at other times flaunted cruelly. However, the church is not meant to be politicized as the world is politicized. It must embody the principles of God's kingdom. But while Christian leaders all agree they are accountable to God, there is less unanimity about whether they should be accountable to those they lead. There are certainly few people who could be more damaging and deadly than Christian leaders who have given place to Satan, especially when they feel themselves to be "under attack."

There are those too who think of accountability primarily in financial terms. Aware of a growing crescendo of public indignation about the irresponsible way some churches and Christian organizations have misused money, they call for measures of financial control. How disgraceful it would be, they protest, if the government had to frame laws to limit Christian corporate sin.

In this chapter as in chapter three, our principle concern is with Christian leaders. For being as human as we are, they may err and sin. Peter and Barnabas played fast and loose with basic gospel truths and were too cowardly to stand up to false teachers. They compromised. Paul had to rebuke them publicly (Gal 2:11-14). Leaders have spiritual needs. They know loneliness and depression. They are exposed to pressures and temptations many of us do not share. They can be tempted by money, by lust, by arrogance or by conceit. Like all of us, leaders not only need the Holy Spirit's faithfulness but also the Spirit's faithfulness _mediated by the body of Christ._

We must not view them as we view public figures, targets for the venomous darts of our criticism. They are our fellow believers. We must build walls of prayer around them. But we must do more. They need overt expressions of our concern. And as we give them, we shall begin to see there are two sides to the coin of accountability, leaders' accountability to God for our spiritual welfare and our accountability to God to be faithful to those leaders who stand in need of our fidelity.

King David was a man exposed to the perils of leadership. Having grown careless and lethargic, he left military responsibility in wartime in the sole custody of Joab, the commander-in-chief of Israel's armed forces. Then tempted by a woman's beauty, David committed adultery. In an attempt to cover his sin he deceived, tried to corrupt and tried to manipulate the woman's husband. Failing in his shabby maneuvers he arranged for the husband's murder, making Joab his accomplice in crime.

So as a God-anointed sovereign, David needed discipline. How was the disciplinary process to be initiated? Would it be designed to humiliate David? to expose him? to protect him from the political consequences of his act? Or was it primarily to restore a relationship between God and David, a relationship that super-seded David's historical role?

How did God discipline David? "The LORD sent Nathan to David" (2 Sam 12:1).

Armed with God's wisdom Nathan caught David off balance. He aroused the king's ire over the story of an injustice done to an impoverished shepherd. As David in rage called God to witness that justice would be done to the perpetrator of the crime, Nathan cried, "You are the man" (2 Sam 12:7). Nathan's words were not exactly a rebuke, but rather a prophetic statement of truth. Truth can be expressed plainly, openly and boldly, yet with humility. An accusation need not represent an attack. Nor was candor born of the same mother as pride. And while it is true that God often gives more shocking words of truth to prophets than to the rest of us, we may all speak truth with loving boldness and simplicity.

The bold words worked. God bore witness to them by taking from David the child conceived by his adultery as well as by altering the whole course of David's life. God's prime goal was to bring to David his reconciling grace. As a result of the discipline, David saw this very thing. "Cast me not away from thy presence, and take not thy holy Spirit from me," he cried. "Restore to me the joy of thy salvation" (Ps 51:11-12).

Some leaders, when faced with the threat of discipline, cry the same words with the same fervor. Yet their concern is adulterated by a fear of exposure and a need to cling to power. Not so David. He knew he could strike no bargains with God. He prayed as a broken man whose first priority was fellowship with God. "Thou hast no delight in sacrifice. . . . The sacrifice acceptable to God is a broken spirit; a broken and contrite heart, O God, thou wilt not despise" (Ps 51:16-17). He was concerned not for his sovereignty, but for the kingdom over which he was sovereign. "Do good to Zion in thy good pleasure; rebuild the walls of Jerusalem" (Ps 51:18).

God's goal was reconciliation. How did he achieve it? Among the means God used was a man, a prophet. We might be tempted to say, "As a prophet Nathan had divine authority, an authority superior even to that of an earthly king. I am not a prophet. So

God will not call me to speak to a leader about his or her sin." But if for a moment you will put yourself in Nathan's shoes, you will realize how much courage was required of him.

God's prophets have been no more immune from the wrath of kings than anyone else. Jesus makes it clear that many of God's messengers were killed by the ancestors of their tomb builders (Lk 11:47-48). Therefore, we must be careful not to ask if we are prophets but ask if we have Nathan's courage to run the risks Nathan ran.

It was a perilous mission. A cornered murderer, especially one with supreme political authority, is dangerous. David was a victim of the same psychological consequences of sin we all experience. He had a need to justify himself, hide from his conscience, to shut out the Holy Spirit's voice. Mere accusation was not enough. Nathan needed God's wisdom as well as boldness. These God confirmed in the events that followed. And he will confirm our own words with power when we truly convey to anyone his message in his way by his Spirit.

One more point before we leave David. Some Christians argue that Christian leaders should never be approached as Nathan approached David. They use the words, "Touch not my anointed ones!" in support of their views. Interestingly, the words were uttered by David himself (1 Chron 16:22; Ps 105:15).

On two occasions in his life David could have killed his persecutor and predecessor Saul. His "touch" could have been the touch of death. However, secure of the promise of God to him that the kingdom would one day be his and recognizing that Saul had been appointed by God, he refused to seize by violence what God had given to another man, who was, for the time being, the anointed king. David would wait God's time.

The situation is hardly analogous to our approaching Christian leaders about their sin. We are not trying to depose the Christian leader. We are certainly not trying to replace him by seizing his power. To use these words to warn against our ministering to our leaders is to create an exaggerated and unbiblical awe of them. It also creates two classes of citizens in the kingdom of God where no division should exist.

In the Local Congregation

In New Testament times the most significant leaders in local churches were elders, men who displayed reliability and certain spiritual qualities. They were drawn commonly (though not exclusively) from among older married men in the congregation. Elders were expected to be able to teach and to exercise pastoral care. The principles that governed the responsibility of first-century Christians toward elders may be taken to apply to relations between leaders and led among Christians universally. Elders were entitled to respect (1 Tim 5:1, 19). Christians were to heed their teaching and follow it. They were to recognize the work leaders carried out, to uphold them in prayer, and where appropriate to support them financially.

But like all leaders, elders could go wrong. And like all led, first-century Christians sometimes entertained critical feelings about elders. They were warned not to rebuke elders but at the same time they were free to speak openly with them about their failings, provided they did so in a proper manner (1 Tim 5:1).

Clearly Paul was not prohibiting confrontation between leaders and led but giving directions about the attitude of those who confronted. In particular he contrasts rebuking with entreating. You _beseech_ someone you love, someone with whom you want to restore an important relationship.

Let us suppose the elder had committed, or was thought to have committed, a serious offense. (Leaders are not only more vulnerable to temptation, but also more exposed to accusations both true and false.) The elder could then be accused (as David had been accused by Nathan), but the accusation was to be made in the presence of witnesses (1 Tim 5:19). In this way the elder would be protected against irresponsible charges and against subsequent inaccurate gossip.

If it is important for all Christians to have the privilege of facing sin in front of a small group of believers before the matter is discussed by the whole congregation, then it becomes more important still when a leader or a leader's sin (or alleged sin) is being considered.

Gossip damages leaders more than the rest of us because gossip flies on wings when it concerns a person in the public eye. The better known and the more widely respected a leader, the more spicy the gossip about the leader and the greater the temptation to spread the gossip. Again the more critical the leader's role in the battle with the powers of darkness, the more strategic his downfall becomes. If the leader does not succumb to temptation, perhaps his or her downfall may be brought about by gossip.

When Leaders Refuse to Bow

Thus Scripture not only holds church leaders accountable for their actions but also calls for ordinary church members to minister to them lovingly and respectfully. Nonetheless, some leaders may resist the charges brought to them. Even when the facts are beyond dispute, leaders sometimes cling both to their power and their self-righteousness. What should be done?

Older denominations and churches have precise disciplinary procedures spelled out. Some of these call for action from someone such as a bishop or from an authoritative body. Yet a hierarchical approach to discipline can be counterproductive as we saw earlier. It lacks the corrective power of discipline by the whole community. The action usually fails to bring about heart searching and purification in the Christian community as a whole. The community is left with its gossip, its hostilities and divisions all intact. Still, hierarchical discipline is better than nothing. If the discipline is carried out in a loving and redemptive way by the peers or superiors whose manifest wish is to help, then such discipline can restore.

Christian churches and organizations abound, however, where pastors, directors and presidents are responsible to nobody but an inactive and intimidated board. In some cases not even a board exists. Even where it does, the board usually realizes that without the dynamism and charisma of the erring leader, the work would collapse, or possibly be replaced by a rival organization headed by their disciplined ex-leader. Often such a leader has walked out of the work with two-thirds of the members of the church or organization. Understandably (but culpably) boards drag their feet.

The Church Boss

Flow charts seldom show where the real power lies. In churches and Christian organizations the pastor or the director may be more of an ornament than a power. Real power vibrates elsewhere. Sometimes there is a tough, older man or woman whom no one has ever dared to cross. The longer such people retain power, the harder they are to remove and the less anyone wants to be involved in dealing with them.

When they first arrived, they were welcomed. At last somebody had come to the church who expressed definite ideas and could get things going. Slowly a "church boss" was entrenched in power. In time conflicts would arise, but they would only serve to establish his or her supremacy. A few aggrieved families might pull out. New people might stop coming. A pall of resentment and deadness would settle on the church. Or the pastor would leave. And two successive pastors would follow, only to pass through successive stages of enthusiasm, bewilderment and dismay before going elsewhere. They were not strong enough to face the church boss, and the church membership would not unite behind the pastor unless he showed himself clear-headed enough to see the issue and strong enough to deal with it.

Dale, a friend of ours who pastors a church in southern California, became interested in and eventually convinced of what we were teaching about corrective church discipline. He began to feature the topic in his preaching and model it in his pastoral care. The results were at times amusing, at times healthful and occasionally dismaying.

The first person to admonish Dale was an old woman who asked him to visit her "for a serious talk." She complained he had responded warmly to her invitations to visit her "sometime" but that the visit had never materialized. Dale saw at once that he had been irresponsible in agreeing thoughtlessly to an open invitation which had meant much to her but less to Dale. He acknowledged his wrong, apologized, and grew more careful about his responses to invitations.

One of the church's elders, Walt, also approached Dale and accused him of sin, the sin of entertaining a call from another church and thus breaking faith with the congregation. Dale was surprised. He understood his call to the congregation was purely of a temporary and problem-solving nature. There had been no written or verbal agreement implying anything else. When Walt refused to accept Dale's protest, Dale suggested he bring two or three others so that they could discuss the matter more fully and find some way of being reconciled. Did the others see the matter in the same way as the elder? But Walt did nothing. The relationship between the two cooled.

Subsequently Walt made a second accusation, this time before the congregation. He accused Dale of being politically (as opposed to pastorally) motivated in his actions in the church. The accusation hurt personally. More importantly, Dale saw public accusations by one leader of another as divisive of the body.

Afterward he approached Walt privately and asked him to substantiate what had been a vague but damaging accusation. Why was he accused of political motivation? Why was Dale not pastorally motivated? Walt reaffirmed his accusations but refused to elaborate on them or to explain his grounds for making them. Dale also asked Walt why he had not come to him privately with his accusation, as he had with the previous one. "Because you wouldn't have listened anyway," was the reply.

Dale said he was still willing to listen further to him, but that to make a serious public accusation first without having tried to deal with the matter privately was sinful. He called on Walt to repent of the manner in which he had made his criticism, even if the content were accurate. The elder's reply: "No way!"

Dale could not let the matter drop. Before him stood a bitter and confused man. Dale would have to bring two or three others to act as witnesses and helpers in bringing about reconciliation. He dreaded Walt's possible intransigence and its consequences. But he could not let those possibilities impede an attempt to seek reconciliation between the two of them.

The next Saturday morning they met with two other elders, Harold and Bob, both of whom were the elder's longstanding friends. After prolonged and open discussion it was clear to Harold and Bob that the church's health depended upon their ability to resolve the issue. They supported Dale and called on Walt to acknowledge his fault and accept pardon for it. But he remained obdurate.

"Then we have no choice but to bring the matter before the congregation," Dale observed. Bob suggested prayer. There was a heavy silence. Then Bob prayed.

Again Walt was asked to repent and receive forgiveness. For several moments he remained silent again. Then he agreed and said he would ask for forgiveness.

It would be tempting at this point to analyze what was taking place in psychological and sociological terms, to discuss the group dynamics, the possible transference and countertransference manifestations. It might also be valuable to do so. But for the present let us note that the three men went immediately to their brother's support. They pronounced his pardon and prayed again with gratitude and praise. Still more to the point, Walt subsequently displayed more flexible thinking and was easier to work with.

Professor Samuel Southard, head of the department of pastoral counseling at Fuller Theological Seminary, describes the case of Mr. Riggs, an intransigent, power-hungry deacon in a local congregation, in his book *Pastoral Authority in Personal Relationships*.[1] Several disheartened pastors had left one after another. Meanwhile church membership declined steadily.

At last a Pastor Long had the courage to face the Riggses in their home one Sunday afternoon. However, he met with such a torrent of abuse that he was unmanned. Unable to preach that evening, Long wept as he reported what had taken place to the small congregation. A committee was formed to speak with Riggs.

Riggs received the committee civilly and solemnly, and spoke earnestly to the committee about the necessity that all of them should search their hearts before God. Chastened, the committee left. But a chance thought made them turn back. Each of them had acknowledged personal unworthiness. But had Riggs or his wife?

Before getting back into their car the men decided to give the Riggses an opportunity to share in the general need for heart searching. It was well that they did. The blast of fury they

encountered showed them clearly where the real evil lay. When the committee reported back to the church, the church unanimously decided to suspend the Riggses from membership until they showed signs of repentance. The deacon sold his home within a week and moved to another town. Southard comments:
1. A few people, like Mr. Long, stood their ground against Mr. & Mrs. Riggs for 15 years. Without them the church would have dissolved. 2. When these people sought help from former pastors, they were told to give in, be quiet, leave or think positive thoughts about the Riggses. 3. Pastor Long was prepared by previous seminary training in a mental hospital to talk openly and deliberately with hostile and suspicious people. Yet even this training was not full protection against Riggs' attack. The understanding fellowship of the congregation was essential for restoration of his confidence and ministry. 4. Twenty years ago, the general practitioner of the community told a Sunday-school teacher that Mrs. Riggs was chronically emotionally disturbed. Yet for almost that length of time, the Midland Church and its pastors tolerated the grossest sort of spiritual pathology in a leadership position. 5. If pastor and church had moved wisely in the past could this couple have been redeemed?[2]

The last question is crucial. People who abuse power are changed progressively as they do so. In abusing power they give themselves over to evil, untruth, self-blindness and hardness without allowing themselves or anyone else to see what is happening. The longer the process continues, the harder repentance becomes. Church bosses must be spotted and rescued early, or they may never be rescued at all. They have caused inconceivable havoc among churches throughout history.

It is important that all Christian leaders be held accountable not only to God, but to those they lead. The principle benefits, and its neglect can harm both leaders and led.

17
An
Approach
to Change

MY WIFE AND I ONCE LIVED IN AN ADOBE house on a hillside over-looking a leper colony in Bolivia. The climate and topography were not unlike parts of New Mexico with dry, semidesert scrub. In front of the house lay a loose clutter of rocks onto which the maid threw the dishwater whenever she had finished with it. One day she threw a pile of watermelon seeds out with the dishwater.

Before long, vines were clambering over the rocks and in time the largest, sweetest watermelons grew and ripened. No effort had been made to cultivate them. Dirty dishwater is not noted for its fertilizing properties. Something about the environment favored the growth of the melons and two people who knew nothing about agriculture were illogically proud of a crop they had not even planted.

Church discipline needs a favorable environment if it is to produce lively, healthy growth. It needs a climate which will influence it in the way the Bolivian foothills influenced the watermelon seeds. Church discipline needs a context.

In this chapter we shall deal with two aspects of that environment, the human aspect and the structural aspect. The human aspect concerns the attitudes of Christians toward their fellow sinners, and in particular their expectations and their willingness to give of themselves. The structural aspect concerns the logistical arrangements in which those attitudes can be expressed.

Our Expectations

A reconciling aim is the product of a warm, self-giving heart. One necessary change in our attitudes, then, will concern our willingness to give of ourselves in the service of others. But warmth needs to be combined with sophistication about evil. Warm naiveté is useless. Yet a biblical difficulty arises. In 1 Corinthians 14:20 Paul states, "Be babes in evil, but in thinking be mature." Is he telling us not to be knowledgeable about human sin?

Not really. Paul is chiding the Corinthians primarily for making idiots of themselves before unbelievers by the indiscrete way they used the gift of tongues in public. His sentence begins, "Brethren, do not be children in your thinking. . . ." A looser translation might be, "Don't be so dumb!"

God does not call us to be babes in our knowledge of human nature. We are too naive about human sinfulness, both inside and outside the church. We tend not to see sin that takes place under our noses, and when we do see it, we react with shock and dismay. We do not expect to find sin because we do not know our own hearts. This constitutes a personal tragedy as well as a church tragedy since we can appreciate God's holiness only to the degree that we understand the depravity of our hearts. And vice versa. We grasp both essences by contrast.

There is a sense in which all spiritual progress is a progress in two directions at once. It is progress into the discovery of the hell of our own corruptness coupled with such a knowledge of God that our shame and horror are forever being turned into wonder, glory and joy. We cannot grasp the love of God unless we see how unlovable we are. But if we do both, the result will be a changed attitude to the sins of others. We may grieve, but we will no longer be shocked. Nor will we feel embarrassed or superior. Our sinfulness may take a different form from that of other people, but we will know it to be every bit as abhorrent.

Our Willingness to Give

A second change in attitude concerns our willingness to give of ourselves to one another. And this in turn is related to the genuineness of our giving of our time and our energy to God. Yet Christ's emphasis seems more on the matter of giving money. Why? Is there some relationship between the two, between the willingness to give of ourselves (our time and our emotional energy) and our willingness to give our money away? Indeed there is. True generosity in one area commonly coincides with generosity in the other. Christian communities where there is generous self-giving are usually those characterized by financial generosity. Both are connected with giving our very persons to God. And while many of us feel we have already given ourselves to God, it may be that we have done so with many unconscious reservations.

Consider how the Macedonian churches gave to the Jerusalem relief fund. Paul describes it to the Corinthians. "We want you to know, brethren, about the grace of God which has been shown in the churches of Macedonia, for in a severe test of affliction, their abundance of joy and their extreme poverty have overflowed in a wealth of liberality on their part. For they gave . . . beyond their means . . . begging us earnestly for the favor of taking part in the relief of the saints—and this, not as we expected, but first they gave themselves to the Lord and to us by the will of God" (2 Cor 8:1-5).

There we have it. Financial generosity, giving oneself to God and giving oneself to others—all mentioned in the same passage. It is not the order in which the three occur that matters. Ideally it should follow the order Paul gives. In real life it may not. But the three belong together.

Four words stand out in the passage. Two concern the circumstances of the Macedonians—*affliction* and *poverty*. Two others concern the way in which they gave—with *joy* and *liberality*.

Moreover, each of these words is qualified. The affliction they endured (whose nature is unclear) was "a severe test." Their poverty was "extreme." On the other hand their joy was in "abundance," and their liberality "overflowed" in its wealth. If we can forget ourselves for a moment and concentrate on the spectacle of these afflicted, impoverished Christians begging "earnestly for the favor of taking part in the relief of the saints," and giving "beyond their means," our hearts will be stirred.

Clearly Paul was reluctant to accept their generosity. Why else would there have been any need for them to beg him? (Can you imagine modern fundraisers protesting because people were giving too much?) Paul would have accepted a smaller gift since he himself had asked them to give. It was the fearful cost of their generosity that would lead him to protest, forcing them to beg him to take all they offered. It would seem that they wanted to share in the very suffering of their brothers and sisters in Jerusalem.

Cultural pressures and childhood traumas may help to explain part of our difficulty in giving, but they do not excuse us. How can we learn to be generous? By first recognizing any lack of generosity we may suffer from and by praying that God will change us. We should study prayerfully and even memorize the last half of Matthew 6. If we do both, we will find that God will begin to confront us with choices, choices that call us to decide between sacrificial giving and playing it safe. At first we may give but not cheerfully. But it will be better to give even so, as an exercise in faith. And the more we learn of the principles of Matthew 6 (not being anxious about physical necessities), the more we live on the raw edge of faith, the more we will experience the faithfulness of God and the more we shall experience joy in giving.

But what of self-giving? That too is related to financial giving. We cannot truly give ourselves to others without first giving ourselves to God. And we cannot give ourselves to God without trusting him about our everyday needs. To give ourselves to him means that we will obey him, and obedience is impossible without trust. Thus self-giving, like financial giving, is intimately related to our trust in God. The result is an environment that nurtures others in the body, creating a context for healthy church discipline.

Structure and Discipline

But the creation of an environment conducive to corrective discipline calls for logistical changes. Self-giving requires a medium of expression. There has to be close social contact between people. Christians need to meet in small groups, indeed to *belong to* small groups and be committed to the other group members. Such groups correspond roughly to families in normal social organization.

We humans act out the drama of our lives on two stages. We play in the intimate theater of the household and on the broad stage of civic life. Most of us have only minor roles on the big stage. We are stars at home but only crowd-scene players in wider society. Yet both roles are important to our growth and emotional health, each contributing special disciplines of human interaction. The one provides the stresses and reassurances of intimacy, the other those of identification with something big and powerful. Both also define our identities, serving as mirrors in which we dimly perceive who and what we are.

We accept the importance of family without question but rarely pause to think of the importance of our civic roles. Yet without both we cease to be fully human. The very fact that we are members of a wider society has an impact on us. Why else would we read the newspaper so avidly?

I am a withdrawn and asocial creature, yet the tides of my being rise willy-nilly with the pull of society. I hate football. Yet I am absurdly and illogically delighted when the Winnipeg Blue Bombers win the Canadian Grey Cup. I am puzzled and a little humiliated to find that I am not immune from popular enthusiasm. I am a crowd-scene player in the civic drama of my city.

Likewise in our Christian lives we need the intimacy of a small fellowship group as well as the larger church community if we are to develop Christian character. But in contrast to our everyday lives, as Christians we tend to pay more attention to the larger body than to the small groups within it. We regard the former as essential, but the latter with suspicion.

Yet over the past thirty years a powerful and still-growing movement of home fellowship groups has revitalized the churches of a wide variety of traditions. Small groups have added zest to teaching, worship, prayer and evangelism and have changed fellowship from an abstraction to a living experience. The proliferation of such groups reflects a deep hunger for intimacy that larger-sized groups cannot meet.

Some of the hunger arises from the very fact that church life is often one-sided. But it is aggravated by social problems created by urbanization, industrialization and technology. The intimacy of even the nuclear family is disappearing as divorce and separation take their toll, and as TV sets suck into their devouring mouths the energies and affections we once reserved for real people.

For too long churches have been obsessed with bigness and growth, and too little aware of their depersonalizing dangers. Large groups can never be the seedbeds of healthy church discipline. If it is to be full-orbed, it must begin in the intimacy, concern and fidelity found in a small fellowship group.

Many books give practical instructions for forming and running small groups. Our own preference is for groups that are mixed in age, sex, educational and social background, that are integrated into a larger church fellowship and that are geographically based. But they will not come into existence easily. They call for thought, prayer and above all a thorough conviction about their place and value. What else can we say to inspire such commitment?

First, no awakening or revival makes an enduring impact on a society without them. Whitefield could probably outpreach Wesley, and may have won more converts in his public meetings, yet Wesley influenced the course of British life more powerfully and for a longer period. The difference did not lie in the numbers of their converts, but in Wesley's organization of his converts into *classes* and *societies*.

The classes, subunits of the societies, consisted of a dozen or so people meeting weekly with their leader to share their spiritual advances and setbacks and to reconcile quarrels and disagreements. The majority of conversions as well as the building of disciples took place in the classes.

Second, small groups that meet in homes or on church premises can provide what may be the only realistic answer to the congregation's pastoral needs. No pastor, however gifted, can care effectively for more than thirty families. If he thinks he can, his delusion arises from his ignorance of the families' real sins and problems.

In his *Reformed Pastor,* Richard Baxter left us an invaluable treatise on pastoral devotion, but its value lies precisely there—in its call to devotion rather than in its practicality. Baxter set aside many hours every week to interviewing families committed to his care. Yet to each family he could give only an hour or so twice a year. Baxter's ardor and commitment should stir us all to zeal, but his model is inadequate.

Third, and here lies the crux of the matter, Christian growth has to be learned, if I may return to the image in chapter one, in the swimming pool. We cannot learn to love people unless we are close enough both for comfort and for inconvenience. Love costs. We cannot heal the wounded unless we are willing to clean away the pus and put up with foul smells. Growth in Christian love calls for the discipline of interacting with unlovable Christian people.

Fourth, fellowship groups can become fertile soil in which new leaders develop and flourish. Whereas exclusive participation in larger activities tends to infantilize and intimidate us, smaller groups entrust members with responsibility and give them confidence as they learn leadership skills because they are more tolerant of mistakes.

Finally, small groups provide the basic environment for both training in godliness and corrective discipline. Small group members have more opportunity to know one another. Personal idiosyncrasies and annoying habits do not take any longer to come to light than positive qualities. If fellowship is to remain warm and living, the negative traits have to be faced and dealt with.

Small fellowship groups will not guarantee these results. Small groups can be totally ineffective. They merely provide the logistical setting in which certain results can take place. But without the setting the results will almost certainly not follow. We can solve logistical problems, organize seminars and create small groups. Yet if we want what we have been talking about, then God will have to bring it to pass. But first he will require at least one person in the church to wait on him in prayer. And if there is to be widespread and genuine change, it can only come with changes in the values, goals and orientation of a majority of church members.

Needless to say, waiting on God and careful planning go together. Robert Culp describes how reform was brought about in a church that had long known bitterness and dissension. The process of thinking through what church was about was a long one, involving a good deal of discussion by the whole church. He writes:

We began with a men's weekend retreat, taking apart several books on the church and spiritual leadership. Then in January, 1980, we launched an "All Church Retreat"—actually a series of events for the entire congregation. We cleared the month's calendar of everything except Sunday morning worship. Instead, we held discussion and sharing sessions twice each week. And twice more each week, the same people met in small groups to work with our purpose, strategy and structure.

It was intense, but by the end of the month, we had hammered out a statement of purpose and some additional methods for implementing it. We honed and polished these things for another three months, until in May we formally voted to suspend the by-laws for six months and try out our concepts. The vote was unanimous.

What our church was really all about, the statement said, was "to be a loving fellowship of committed believers worshipping together, seeking to reconcile persons to Christ, mature them in him, and involve them in ministry to one another and the world." We followed this with a list of our four main strategies: celebrating together, demonstrating koinonia, witnessing and discipling.

This meant reorganizing our church according to our purpose. Organizations and activities were no longer justified just because of tradition. The question was: Are they consistent with our mission? Do they help us get the job done?

When the dust had settled, we no longer had a men's organization, a women's organization, a board of Christian education, or a board of trustees. Their functions were either swallowed up elsewhere or found to be unnecessary. And there was very little opposition. Most leaders wanted a change. A few of them had second thoughts when they found themselves no longer in leadership positions. When three adult choirs were merged into one, some leaders felt left out and told me so. But they were not bitter; they were just struggling to find new places of service. And with time they found them.[1]

Notice that with new purposes old functions became irrelevant. Notice also that some people with fulfilling jobs found themselves temporarily without leadership positions. Significant change cannot come about without tension. Old institutions do not always succumb to annihilation gracefully, nor do people like giving up offices in which they find gratification.

Most churches are as cluttered as an attic with unnecessary boards, committees, organizations and functionaries. Yet change means change. Old traditions have vigorous death throes. And when human carnality is involved, bitterness can arise. But unless change comes, unless a church environment conducive to healthy discipline can be created in a church, a wineskin problem will follow.

Battle for Change

Ken and I realized before we ever decided to write a book about church discipline that the big problem would be how to get from A to B, that is, how churches could become the sort of churches where discipline could and would take place helpfully. It must be clear from what I have written in this chapter that for many churches getting from A to B will be no small task. Neither attitudinal nor organizational changes take place easily.

Anything worthwhile costs. In part one of this book we asserted that to ignore church discipline is more costly than to reinstitute it. But this does not negate the reality of the conflict that will be involved in reviving it. And like kings going to war or people building towers, we are advised to count costs before we start. Therefore, look well at the situation in your church and do not for a moment minimize the difficulty of changing long-established attitudes and structures. To fail to do so at the outset is to invite discouragement, and perhaps disaster later on.

Opponents, critics and fence-sitters will not be wanting. How could it be otherwise? And while psychology and sociology can give us interesting explanations for their reactions, there is always a more sinister reason. The powers of hell oppose church discipline and will fight it tooth and nail. They will exploit our doubts and fears for their own grim ends, using weak and carnal Christians as their dupes and agents. Whoever seeks to re-establish church discipline automatically awakens hell's vitriolic hostility.

Church members are those who have been "delivered . . . from the domain of darkness, and transferred . . . to the kingdom of [God's] beloved Son" (Col 1:13 NASB). Church discipline is needed because Satan does not willingly relinquish his erstwhile captives. He seeks to renew his control. Refusing to recognize either his overthrow by the rule of Christ or the claims of Christ on his followers, he proudly reasserts his own rule, reawakening and reviving the sinful patterns of the past. And only when a champion dares to stand where Christ stands and to confront Satan's fraudulent claims, only then will change come about.

How else can we explain the present situation? Is Christ enthroned? Was he not manifested that he might destroy the works of the devil (1 Jn 3:8)? Yet if he is both enthroned and conqueror, I can suggest only one explanation for the current situation. Champions are lacking who are jealous for the authority of the kingdom of Jesus and prepared to do battle as they drive hell's vultures from picking at the living flesh of Christ's redeemed.

But such champions will need to see the battle as it is. They will have to perceive fence-sitters and opponents of discipline as hell's dupes. Dupes and middle-of-the-roaders may be culpable, but they call more for compassion than for condemnation. If they arouse hostility in us, we are not reacting as true champions of the kingdom or seeing reality as Scripture sees it. Our hostility is to be directed at hell and sin. Unless we can see beyond the human dynamics of the situation to the spiritual conflict in the heavenlies, we shall fight neither in a right spirit nor with unfettered vigor.

Yet how pathetically myopic we are! We see neither God's great hand nor the sinister machinations of the devil. Our view of reality differs little from that of the world around us. We call ourselves theists, believers in a God-created universe. We repeat theological formuli about human sin and Satanic rule, but hasten to add that God still has the upper hand. Christ, we say, has won the victory.

Yet it seems as though Christ stands impotent before the present proliferation of apathy and sin in his church, for we refuse to see. The devil (invisible and politely ignored) goes about his damnable work, buttressing the present church systems with antiquated organizational structures that pander to vanities and egos. It is a bewildering thought—Christ's sword is sheathed while the devil stalks unheeded among us.

It is time we woke up. Christ was indeed manifested. He did destroy the works of the devil. We need put up with Satan's schemes no longer. As followers of Christ we have authority to unleash his conquering sword, joining him in the completion of his devil-destroying conquest.

Our book is a challenge to gird on armor and draw swords. It is a plea to stop playing at church, to set aside personal ambition and the pursuit of personal comfort and to take risks. It would be better to fight and lose than to allow the present situation to continue.

But there is no reason why we should lose. We are invited to run, sword in hand, in the steps of a conqueror.

Appendix

Binding
and Loosing

John Howard Yoder

Better a frank word of reproof than the love that will not speak;
Faithful are the wounds of a friend. Proverbs 27:5-6 (Moffatt)

A study outline is intentionally a skeleton, unevenly filled out. It is not written for smooth and easy reading nor for completeness and balance. The careful reader, evaluating it as an essay, will find the presentation fragmentary. The theologically alert reader will resent the absence of efforts to relate to the range of current schools of thought. Critical questions are avoided. Texts are taken literally in a way that may seem naive. "How-to-do-it" concerns are mixed with the meaning of atonement with no respect for pigeonholing. No energy has been invested in explaining how this simplification differs from fundamentalism in method or motive.

The position suggested here may seem to gather together the dangers of several ecclesiastical scarecrows. It gives more authority to the church than does Rome, trusts more to the Holy Spirit than does Pentecostalism, has more respect for the individual than humanism, makes moral standards more binding than puritanism, is more open to the given situation than the "new morality." If practiced it would change the life of churches more fundamentally than has yet been suggested by the perennially popular discussions of changing church structures.

Thus the path to the rediscovery of Christian faithfulness may lead right through some positions modern Christian "moderates" have been trying to avoid. The concern expressed here does not fit at any one point on the "map" of traditional denominational positions—which may just show that something is wrong with the map. The positions taken will seem strange to Christians of many schools of thought—and yet it echoes a conviction historically present in many Christian traditions.

In leaving to one side other aspects of the problem of church renewal, and in opening up this one particular topic in this simple, generally accessible, apparently dogmatic way, I imply no claim that oversimplification is generally a way to solve problems. The naive form is a discussion-starting method and not a theological stance.

I. The Key Text—Matthew 18:15-20

15 If your* brother sins
go reprove him
between you* and him alone;
if he listens
you* have won your* brother;

16 if he does not listen
take with you* one or two more
so that "by the mouth of two or three witnesses
every matter may be established (Deut. 19:15)";

17 if he will not listen to them
tell the church;
if he will not listen even to the church
let him be to you* as a gentile and a tax collector.

18 Truly I say to you†
what you† bind on earth stands bound in heaven
and what you† loose on earth stands loosed in heaven.

19 Again I say to you†
that if two of you agree on earth
concerning every matter for which they ask
it shall be done for them by my father in heaven;

20 for where two or three are gathered in my name,
there I am in their midst.

*in verses 15-17 the words _you_ and _your_ and the imperative verb are all singular.
†in verses 18-19 _you_ and the related verbs are all plural.

Discussion questions on Matthew 18:15-20.
Note your first impressions of the passage under consideration before
continuing with further study.

☐ What is the purpose of dealing with a brother in this way?

☐ Is this way of dealing with a brother the responsibility of every Christian? Of
the one sinned against? Of church officers?

☐ What do you take "binding" and "loosing" in verse 18 to mean?

☐ Can you think of other New Testament texts on this subject or is it an isolated
idea?

☐ Has this practice that Jesus describes here been a part of your experience as
a Christian?

II. The Twofold Meaning of *Binding* and *Loosing*

In the sweeping summary authorization which he gives the church, Jesus uses
the verbs *bind* and *loose* in a way which takes for granted that their meaning is
clear to his listeners. Centuries later, when neither secular nor religious usage
has retained the pair of terms, we must resurrect their meaning. Perhaps the very
fact that the terms no longer have a customary sense in current language may
permit us to use them now as a "technical" label for the practice Jesus commanded.

A. *Two aspects of meaning.* There are clearly two aspects to the meaning of these
verbs:

(1) Forgiveness: to "bind" is to withhold fellowship, to "loose" is to forgive.
This is supported by the parallel texts in Luke 17:3 (based in turn on Lev 19:17;
note the other elements in Lk 17:14 which are also parallel to Mt 18:14 and 18:21-
22) and in John 20:25. It is supported as well by the other portions of Matthew
18 (10-14, the hundredth sheep; 21-22, seventy times seven; 23-35, the unmerciful
servant).

(2) Moral discernment: To "bind" is to enjoin, to forbid or make obligatory;
to "loose" is to leave free, to permit. We recognize the root *ligare* "to bind" in
obligate, ligament, league. Thus the New English Bible translates "forbid" and
"allow."

This was the current, precise technical meaning which the terms *bind* and *loose*
(i.e., their Aramaic equivalents) probably had in the language of the rabbis of
Jesus' time. Moral teaching and decision making in Judaism took the form of
rulings by the rabbis on problem cases brought to them, either "binding" or
"loosing" depending on how they saw the Law applying to each case (cf. below
XIII/A).

Out of these decisions there accumulated a fund of precedents and principles,
called the *halakah,* the moral tradition, which continued from one generation
to the next to be useful in relating the Law to current problems. By taking over
these terms from rabbinic usage, Jesus assigns to his disciples an authority to
bind and loose previously claimed only by the teachers in Israel.

This dimension of meaning is the one emphasized in the parallel phrasing of Matthew 16:19, and is further confirmed when we look at Matthew 18:15-20 more closely. Verses 15-17, describing the direct dealings with the brother, are spoken in the singular; but the following verses shift to the plural. This suggests that the authorization of 18-20 may have a broader import for the church than that of the immediate disciplinary context.

B. *The relation of forgiveness and discernment.* At first sight these two activities would seem to not be closely related; yet on closer analysis their intimate interrelation becomes clear:

(1) Forgiving presupposes prior discernment. Jesus' words startle the modern reader with the simplicity of his beginning: "If your brother sins . . ." In our age of tolerance and confusion we are not used to thinking of "sin" as that easily identifiable. Jesus assumes that the moral standards by which sin is to be identified are knowable and known. He further assumes that the offender and those who reprove him share a common moral yardstick.

(2) Forgiving furthers discernment. If the standards appealed to by those who would reprove someone are inappropriate, the best way to discover this is through the procedure of person-to-person conversation with reconciling intent. Thus the group's standards can be challenged, tested and confirmed, or changed as is found necessary in the course of their being applied. The result of the process, whether it ends with the standards being changed or reconfirmed, is to record a new decision as part of the common background of the community, thus accumulating further moral insights by which to be guided in the future.

(3) Discernment necessitates forgiveness. There is in every serious problem a dimension of personal offense or estrangement. This is the case even when the issue at stake is quite "impersonal" or "technical" or "objective." Therefore, in every right decision there must be an element of reconciliation. The idea that questions of right and wrong could best be studied somehow "objectively" or "disinterestedly" is in itself an unrealistic misunderstanding of the personal character of every decision-making process.

(4) Forgiving concern sets the limits of our responsibility for one another's decisions. If I am a Christian at all, what I do is my brother's and my sister's business. We owe one another counsel and, sometimes, correction and pardon. Yet it is neither possible nor desirable for my brother to be concerned with all that I do. What then is the point where the search for a common mind ends, and individual variation and personal responsibility begins?

The most current answer is that big sins are the church's business and small ones are not. Yet every effort to draw that line leads to legalism, to concern with the deed rather than the doer, with guilt rather than restoration.

The correlation of the two concerns of forgiveness and discernment provides another answer, though not an abstract one, to this question. Differences of conviction and behavior are unacceptable *when they offend.* The "line" is not drawn theoretically but in terms of personality and interpersonal concern. If the difference destroys fellowship, it is for that reason a topic for reconciling concern. Any variance not dealt with, on the grounds that it is unimportant, becomes increasingly important with the passage of time. Unattended, it magnifies the next conflict as well.

But if on the other hand Christians have been accustomed to dealing with one another in love, and have been finding that they are able to be reconciled whenever they deal with a matter in love, they find as well that their "tolerance threshold" rises—that is, a spirit of mutual trust arises in which fewer differences offend.

Thus both the necessity of dealing with some differences, and the possibility of leaving other matters to individual liberty, are rooted in the very process of the reconciling approach to the brother.

"Forgiveness" and "discernment" do not point to two alternative meanings of the same words, whereby one would always need to choose which meaning applies. Forgiveness and discernment are not two poles of a tension but two sides of a coin. Each presupposes and includes the other. In the following pages we shall deal predominantly with the "forgiveness" face of the coin, but never as if this excluded the other aspect of moral discernment.

Discussion questions on the meaning of binding and loosing.

☐ Can you be deeply reconciled with your brother or sister while disagreeing on moral decisions?

☐ Can you tolerate more disagreement with someone you have forgiven or who has forgiven you?

☐ Can you agree on moral issues with someone you have not forgiven? Are you more critical of someone you have not forgiven?

☐ Before reading further, note your first reactions on reading that Jesus authorizes his disciples: a) to forgive sins; and b) to make binding moral decisions.

☐ What place has forgiveness had until now in your concept of what the church is for in your experience of Church?

III. The Source of the Authority to Bind and Loose

A. *The authority given the church is parallel to the authority of Christ himself* (Jn 20:19-23). Throughout Jesus' ministry, especially as recorded in the fourth Gospel, Jesus scandalized the authorities by his claims to have been sent by the Father in a unique way (5:18ff., 6:30ff., 7:28ff., 8:36ff., 10:25ff.). "Just as the Father sent me, so I send you."

If it was possible to be yet more offensive to official reverence, it was when Jesus took it upon himself to forgive sins (Mk 2:7; Lk 7:48ff.); yet this is what the disciples are charged to do. He lays upon them, and thereby upon us, the same power he claimed for himself.

B. *The scandal of the divine mandate.* We do not fully understand the grandeur of this commission if we are not first, as were Jesus' contemporaries, shocked by it. Not only were the contemporary Jews shocked (Mk 1:7, they called it blasphemy); Protestants are too. Reacting against the abuses of Roman Catholic penitential practice (see below, section IX/E), Protestants have for centuries been arguing that "only God can forgive," and that the believer receives reassurance of forgiveness not from another man, but in the secret of his own heart.

The heat and vigor of this old Protestant-Catholic debate point us to the difficulty we have in conceiving, and in believing, that God really can authorize ordinary humans to commit him, that is, to forbid and to forgive on his behalf with the assurance that the action stands "in heaven." How can it be, and what can it mean, that such powers are placed in the hands of ordinary men the likes of Peter? The jealous concern of religious leaders, and of all religion, for the transcendence of God, for his untouchability and his distance from us, might have been able to adjust, or to make an exception, for arrogant claims like this made on behalf of some most exceptional man, a high priest or a grand rabbi, a prophet or king. But the real scandal of the way God chose to work among humans—what we call the Incarnation—is that it was an ordinary working man from Nazareth who commissioned a crew of ordinary people—former fishermen and taxgatherers—*to forgive sins.*

C. *The church is empowered by the Holy Spirit.* The text in John 20 links the imparting of the Holy Spirit directly with the commission to forgive. According to John 14:16, the functions of the promised Spirit will be to "convince," to "lead into all truth," and to remind believers of teachings of Jesus which they had not grasped before.

In Acts 1 and 2 the function of the Spirit is to empower the disciples to be witnesses; but in the rest of the story of Acts, notably in the decisions of chapters 13 and 15, but also in the modest details of Paul's travel arrangements, the Spirit is active especially in making decisions. If the proportionate space given to various themes is indicative, the basic work of the Holy Spirit is to guide in discernment, with prophecy, testimony, inward conviction, and empowerment for obedience being subordinate aspects of that work.

The promise of the presence of Christ "where two or three are gathered in my name" is often understood in modern Protestantism as meaning either that there are grounds for the efficacy of prayer or that the gathered congregation may sense a spiritual presence in their midst. Yet in the original context of Matthew 18:19-20 its application is to the consensus (the verb is *sunphonein,* from which we get *symphony*) reached by the divinely authorized process of decision. The "two or three others" are the witnesses required in the Mosaic law for a judicial proceeding to be formally valid (Deut 17:6; 19:15; applied in Num 35:30; 2 Cor 13:1; 1 Tim 5:19; Heb 10:28).

D. *This mandate makes the church the church.* The Greek word *ekklesia* ("church") is found only twice in the Gospels coming from Jesus' lips; the two times are the two "bind and loose" passages. The word *ekklesia* itself (like the earlier Hebrew term, and the Aramaic equivalent which Jesus probably used) does not refer to a specifically religious meeting nor to a particular organization; rather it means the "assembly," the gathering of a people into a meeting for deliberation or for a public announcement.

It is no accident that in Matthew 16, the assignment by Jesus of the power to bind and loose follows directly upon Peter's first confession of Christ as Messiah. The confession is the basis of the authority; the authorization given is the seal upon the confession. The church is where, because there Jesus is confessed as Christ, men and women are empowered to speak to one another in God's Name.

Discussion questions on the church's authorization.
☐ Are there many different activities, or only a few, which Jesus specifically ordered the church to carry out in his name?
☐ Read John 16 and the story in Acts to check on the statements made in section C, above, concerning the work of the Holy Spirit.
☐ What teaching do you remember in the past about who can forgive sin?

IV. The Way of Dealing with the Brother Is Determined by the Reconciling Intent

A. *The reconciling approach is personal.* The entire section 18:15-18 is in the singular: it is a command to the individual. The point of the passage is not that there must be just three steps (rather than four or five) but that: (1) the first encounter is "between the two of you alone"; and that (2) still another small group effort at mediation is made, if the first attempt has failed, before the matter becomes public.

The personal approach first of all guarantees that the matter remains confidential. This is the scriptural prohibition of gossip and defamation. Anyone knows that there is something wrong with talebearing. But sometimes one may think it wrong only because it reveals secrets, or only when the reports one passes on are not true, or when the intention in passing them on is to hurt someone. Each of these explanations of what is wrong with gossip leaves a loophole. Each would permit some kinds of talking about the neighbor's faults to continue.

But if Jesus' command is that the thing to do with an unfavorable report is to go to the person herself/himself, then all one's temptations to pass the word along are blocked, and confidentiality is demanded by the concern for the offender.

Second, it is hereby assured that the process is closely bound to the local situation. Either party can bring into the discussion aspects of the picture which would not be taken into account in general statements of rules. Thus there is a safeguard against the danger of puritanism, which promulgates ethical generalities apart from the context where they must apply, and then applies them strictly and uniformly to every case.

When dealing personally with the offender, in view of his problems, it is not possible to identify as virtues or vices whole categories of behavior without taking part with him in the struggle and the tension of applying them to his situation. It is he who must determine how to behave when he really faces the difficult choice. It may be that the one accused will be able to demonstrate that the action criticized as "sin" was right after all. Or perhaps the one admonishing may be able to help the accused find a better solution he had not seen.

This is a built-in way to assure that churches will not continue to proclaim rules which are no longer capable of application. Standards must constantly be tested by whether it is possible to show the brother how he has sinned. If no one can show him how he should have done differently, then the rules are inadequate and he has been accused unfairly. The very process of conversation with him is then the way to change the rules. If on the other hand the standards continue to be correct, it is in the conversation with the tempted brother that the church will be obliged to give the most fruitful attention to finding other ways of meeting his needs and the temptations which led him to fall.

Yet at the same time that puritanism must be avoided, there is an equal danger of letting the situation provide its own rules. What modern writers call "situation ethics" or "relevance" or "contextualism" may mean simply allowing every individual full liberty to make his own decisions. This approach ends by sacrificing all moral bindingness and all community by adopting in advance, in a general way, a general "rule-against-rules." Binding and loosing achieves the same flexibility to fit each context, without being too sweepingly permissive.

The approach is made in a "spirit of meekness" (Gal 6:1); that is, in recognition of the mutual need of all members for one another and for forgiveness. "Bearing one another's burdens" in Galatians 6:2 is centered not on economic needs, as it is often read, but on the need for this kind of mutual moral support.

B. *Everyone in the church shares responsibility for the reconciling approach.* (1) The command of Matthew 18 assigns the initiative to anyone aware of the offense. The words "against thee," present in most older translations, are missing in the most reliable ancient manuscripts; no such limitation is present in Luke 17:3, Galatians 6:1-2, James 5:19-20.

Those who interpret the instructions to apply only to the person sinned against would shift the attention from the offender's need for reconciliation, to the resentment of the person hurt, in order to give vent to his feelings. If this shift is taken seriously, it means that for certain sins where there is no one specific person offended, or the offended person is absent, there would be nothing for anyone to do. Such a limiting interpretation would also lead the more "mature" or "tolerant" or "accepting" person to absorb the offense and suffer without response, claiming to be adult enough or magnanimous enough not to need to "blow off steam." However, according to Galatians 6, it is the spiritually mature person who is especially responsible to act in reconciliation.

(2) The instructions of Matthew 5:23ff. assign the same responsibility to the person who has offended, if he becomes aware of the offense. His obligation to be reconciled is prior to any other righteous works, however worthy. If your brother has something against you, don't bring your sacrifice to the altar. It is thus the responsibility of every person—of the offender, of the offended, of every informed third party in the Christian fellowship—when aware of any kind of offense, to take initiative toward the restoration of fellowship.

(3) There is no indication that this responsibility belongs in any particular way to "the ministry." "Forgiving" is never indicated in the New Testament as one of the "gifts" distributed within the congregation, nor as a specific responsibility of the pastor, elder, bishop or deacon.

Now there are good common-sense reasons for assuming that anyone who is responsible for leadership in the life of the church will also be concerned for the proper exercise of this reconciling discipline. Thus church leaders might well be included among the "two or three" of Matthew 18:16, or the "wise among you" of 1 Corinthians 6:5, who seek to mediate in the second effort, or among the "more spiritual" of Galatians 6:1. Nevertheless, these are only relative, common-sense considerations. They may be properly applied only after the first attempt at reconciliation: for to inform church leaders before that first attempt is counter to the letter and the intent of the demand for initial confidentiality: "between you and him alone."

For the pastor, the teacher, the elder, the preacher or the deacon to be normally or exclusively the disciplinarian, to the extent that others no longer share with him in the same burden, undermines both the reconciling process and this person's other leadership ministries.

C. *This process belongs in the church.* The church's responsibility may not be turned over to the state (as in the age of the Reformation, according to the convinced theological opinions of Huldreich Zwingli and his followers), or to any other agency representing the total society.

Something like this is happening in our society. Though puritanism in churches is out of style, we are accustomed to the FBI and the draft board exercising moral oversight; we expect schools and social workers to develop the character of the persons they work with.[1]

Nor can the reconciling process in the church be properly replaced by secular psychotherapy.

This study makes no attempt to investigate the complex interrelationships between the church and the mental health institution, between moral guilt and psychotic anxiety, etc. There clearly can and should be no fixed wall between mental health and the church, yet neither may one be absorbed into the other. No definition of the interrelation of these areas can be accepted which takes the matter of guilt and grace completely away from the congregation, or which excludes conscious confession and forgiveness for known willful offenses, or which dissolves all moral measurement into self-adjustment. Not psychiatry and psychology, but the caricature of these professions as secular agencies of forgiveness is the abuse we need to avoid.

D. *Reconciliation and restoration is the only worthy motive.* Any textbook discussion of "church discipline" aligns several other reasons for its application by the church:

☐ the purity of the church as a valuable goal in its own right;

☐ protecting the reputation of the church before the outside world;

☐ testifying to the righteous demands of God;

☐ dramatizing the demands of church membership, especially to new or young members, assumed more likely to be tempted;

☐ safeguarding against relativization and the loss of common Christian moral standards.

Real as they are as by-products and logical as they may well be in motivating the church, it is striking that these concerns are not part of the New Testament picture. These reasonings all put the church in a posture of maintaining her righteousness, whereas the New Testament speaks of shared forgiveness.

Nevertheless there is, beyond Jesus' simple "you will have won your brother," one deeper way of phrasing the motivation. 1 Corinthians 5:6ff. speaks of the discipline process in the image of "leaven": the church is the lump of dough, all of which will be caused to ferment by the presence of a few yeast cells within it. Paul thus says that there is a kind of moral solidarity linking all the members of the body, so that if individuals persist in disobedience within the fellowship, their guilt is no longer the moral responsibility of those individuals alone but becomes a kind of collective blame shared by the whole body. I should deal with my brother's sin because he and I are members one of another; unless I am the agent of his sharing in restoration, he is the agent of my sharing guilt.

Discussion questions on the reconciling approach.

☐ Would it be possible to maintain self-righteousness or judgmental attitudes if the principle of going directly to the offender were respected?

☐ Would the concern for discipline be more effectively taken care of if it were assigned to one particular officer in the church?

☐ Are there certain kinds of questions to which the instructions of Matthew 18 should not apply? Certain sins which should not be so easily forgiven? Or certain others which do not call for this much attention?

V. The Centrality of This Forgiving Function in the New Testament

A. *Reference to "binding and loosing"* occurs at the only places in the Gospels where the word "church" is reported as used by Jesus. The church is therefore most centrally defined as the place where "binding and loosing" takes place. Where this does not happen, "church" is not fully present.

B. *This is the only connection* in which it is said of the church that she is authorized to "commit God." "What you bind on earth stands bound in heaven." The image is that of the ambassador plenipotentiary or of the "power of attorney"; the signature of the accredited representative binds the one who gave the commission.

C. *It is in the context* of this activity of the church that the promise is given (Mt 18:19-20; Jn 14:26; 16:12ff., 20-23) that Christ (or the Spirit) is present where his followers meet in his name. It can be argued that in the New Testament the gift of the Spirit is more often spoken of in connection with discerning and forgiving than (as in Acts 1:8) in relation to witnessing.

D. *This practical application* of forgiveness (18:15-18) is the center of the teaching of the entire chapter 18 on forgiveness.

E. *The only condition* in the Lord's Prayer (Mt 6:12) and the only commentary of Jesus on the Prayer (Mt 6:15) both limit God's forgiveness to those who forgive others (also said in Mt 18:35; Mk 11:25; Eph 4:32; Col 3:13).

F. *The reconciliation* with one's brother or sister is prerequisite to valid worship (Mt 5:23f.).

G. *The promise* of the presence of the Holy Spirit is related especially closely to binding and loosing as we saw above (III/C. Mt 18:19, 20).

H. *It is a function* of the "spiritual" persons on the church, that in a spirit of meekness they restore offenders; this is called "bearing one another's burdens" (Gal 6:1-2). It is also described as "covering a multitude of sins" (Jas 5:19-20).

Discussion questions on the New Testament.

☐ Do you see in the passages cited any localizing of this function as a "ministry" of specific officers of the church?

☐ Do you see in the narrative elements of the New Testament that this function was exercised?

☐ Do you see in the letters of the New Testament that the writer "admonishes" his readers in this way?

☐ As you pray the Lord's Prayer does the phrase "as we forgive" draw your mind to whether you are in fact forgiving others as you ask to be forgiven?

VI. The Centrality of Binding and Loosing in the Life of Free-Church Protestantism

A. *The small group of followers* of Huldreich Zwingli who later came to be known as Anabaptists are usually thought of as having begun their search for the form of the faithful church around the question of the state church or around infant baptism. It is however just as correct to say that the point at which the group of brethren became conscious of its identity was a concern for dealing with offenders according to the pattern of Matthew 18. The term *rule of Christ* with which they referred to the instructions of Matthew 18, was already a fixed phrase in their vocabulary in 1524, before they had reached any final conclusions about the form of the church, the practice of adult baptism or the church's independence from the state.

The first Anabaptists did not say that infants should not be baptized because they cannot have an experience of faith and the new birth, nor did they reject infant baptism only because there was no biblical text commanding it. Their belief was rather that one who requests baptism submits to the mutual obligation of giving and receiving counsel in the congregation; this is what a child cannot do.

In the first clear statement rejecting infant baptism, in September 1524, before going on to discuss whether water has a saving effect or whether unbaptized children are lost, Conrad Grebel wrote "even an adult is not to be baptized without Christ's rule of binding and loosing." Thus the issue is not the age of the one baptized, but the commitment he makes, entering into the covenant community with a clear understanding of its claims upon him.

Balthasar Hubmaier, the theologian of Anabaptism and the only first-generation leader to have the opportunity to draw up printed patterns of church order, likewise put the commitment-character of baptism at the center of his view of reformation. It is clear in his catechism:

Q. What is the baptismal pledge?

A. It is a commitment which one makes to God publicly and orally before the church, in which he renounces Satan, and his thoughts and works. He pledges as well that he will henceforth set all his faith, hope and trust alone in God, and direct his life according to the divine Word, in the power of Jesus Christ our Lord, and in case he should not do that, he promises hereby to the church that he desires virtuously to receive fraternal admonition from her members and from her, as is said above.

Q. What power do those in the church have over one another?

A. The authority of fraternal admonition.

Q. What is fraternal admonition?

A. The one who sees his brother sinning goes to him in love and admonishes him fraternally and quietly that he should abandon such sin. If he does so he has won his soul. If he does not, then he takes two or three witnesses with him and admonishes him before them once again. If he follows him, it is concluded, if not, he says it to the church. The same calls him forward and admonishes him for the third time. If he now abandons his sin, he has saved his soul.

Q. Whence does the church have this authority?

A. From the command of Christ, who said to his disciples, "all that you bind on earth shall be bound also in heaven and all that you loose on earth shall also be loosed in heaven."

Q. But what right has one brother to use this authority on another?

A. From the baptismal pledge in which one subjects oneself to the Church and all her members according to the word of Christ.[2]

Far from being the extreme expression of individualism, the baptism of believers is thus the foundation of the most sweeping communal responsibility of all members for the life of all members.

B. *The Wesleyan revival* may stand as a sample for the numerous renewal movements since the sixteenth century. Wesley and his colleagues had some particular doctrinal emphases, and some unique personal gifts. Their ministry came at a time of great need. Yet the fundamental local experience which the "methodist" had week by week, and the real reason for the movement's practical success, was the regular encounter with the "class." This was a circle of persons meeting regularly, committed to one another and bearing one another's burdens in every way, with special attention to reproof and restoration.

This has been true of movements of revival and renewal in every age; they restore a new freedom in forgiving relationships within the local fellowship, and a renewed ethical earnestness, born not out of rigorous law but out of mutual concern.

C. *Contemporary examples* may be found in the revivalism of Keswick and of East Africa. By the nature of the case such movements, without fixed denominational authority, are open to various organizational, doctrinal and personal peculiarities. Some of these are novel and some perhaps may be questionable. Yet what keeps these movements alive and lively is the renewed experience of the gift of openness, the capacity given by grace to be transparent with the brother about one's own sins and the brother's and thereby to make concrete the assurance of forgiveness.

Thus every revival and every renewal movement has begun by re-establishing among estranged brethren, by repentance, a possibility of communication which had been broken off by the pride and the power-hunger of those within the churches. This kind of renewal may happen at any time or place, and within any kind of Christian group; but for the free churches it is constitutive, it defines their specific character. The free church is not simply an assembly of individuals with a common spiritual experience of personal forgiveness received directly from God; nor is it merely a kind of working committee, a tool to get certain kinds of work carried out. The church is also, as a social reality right in the midst of the world, that people through whose relationships God makes forgiveness visible.

Discussion questions on the histories of renewal.

☐ What has been the record of breakthrough experiences of forgiveness and dialogical discernment in the history of your own community? In the biographies and novels you have read?

☐ What has been the place of failure to dialogue reconcilingly in the failures to "be Church" which you have seen?

VII. The Congregational Method of Decision Making
The mandate to forgive and to decide makes no formal prescriptions about how

small or large groups (the "two or three with you," or "the church") are to discuss and decide. Shall the decisions for the group be made by authority personages, entitled by age or ordination to speak for all? Or by a numerical majority? This question applies not only to "discipline" but to other kinds of "discerning" decision making as well.

This study does not seek to go deeply into this formal matter.

A. *From the narrower realm* of the forgiving process, we must carry over into the broader discussion of churchly decision making several elements which are not usually emphasized in discussions of church organization: (1) the abiding awareness that all decision involves elements of conflict and resentment which need to be dealt with in an atmosphere of abiding forgiveness; and (2) the situation-bound movement of an issue from the two through the few to the congregation.

B. *From the few descriptions* of congregational meetings we have in the New Testament, especially 1 Corinthians 12—14, it seems clear that every member has a right, perhaps a duty, to share in the process. This is not to say that the Corinthian type of church life, charismatically effervescent to the border of disorder, is normative in any formal way.

C. *It is clear that specific "gifts"* contribute to the Spirit-led decision process; it is an orderly and not a formless movement. Some "prophesy," others "preside" and "oversee" and "administer."

D. *The decision process,* although it is often "illuminated" by some immediate inspiration, cannot go forward validly in a knowledge vacuum. There must be, if a decision is to be faithful, a way of informing it with full access to the biblical and theological heritage of Christian insight. If it is to be relevant, it must be equally informed about all the factual dimensions of the current problem. There is no basis for any dichotomy between "religious" and "secular" information, as if either could make decision making superfluous or as if Spirit guidance could get along without either. Holy Spirit guidance is not an alternative to correct information.

Discussion questions on decision making.

☐ Does it ever happen that "religious knowledge" is held to settle a question so that no decision is needed?

☐ Does the same thing ever happen with "secular" knowledge? Do the "authorities" or the "law" settle a question without decision making?

☐ Do current ways of assigning tasks to individuals in our churches reflect the teaching of Romans 12, Ephesians 4, 1 Corinthians 12?

VIII. Misunderstandings of the Concept of "Discipline"

As central as is the commission to bind and to loose, both in the New Testament and in any sober view of the mission of the church, it has nevertheless been widely misunderstood, distorted and neglected. How can this have come about?

So universal a loss of so fundamental a function must be understood and evaluated. Otherwise we may well fall into the same traps and be unable to recover it, or, having grasped it, rapidly lose it again. We shall therefore have to devote a sizable part of our study to the encounter with other points of view.

We look first at misunderstandings connected to the word *discipline*, the label by which this work of brotherhood is most often designated.

A. *The attention may move from the reconciliation of the offender to his punishment.* Under this misunderstanding, instead of restoration, one seeks to inflict on the guilty party some suffering to compensate for the suffering he has caused; at least the suffering of public humiliation. This may be thought of as a right, or a need of the offended persons or group for some kind of vengeance; or it may be thought that the "moral order" somehow demands it, or that the guilty one himself needs chastisement.

B. *The attention may move from the person to the offense.* Big offenses call for big punishment, small ones for lesser measures. These standards are the same regardless of the person involved. Concern for "fairness," that is, uniformity in application, replaces the unpredictability of dealing with one offense at a time.

C. *Concern may move from the offender to the "standards."* Strict observance of the rules is thought of as necessary to reassure the group of its righteousness, or to teach other members the seriousness of the offense, or to testify to the surrounding world of the church's seriousness. The brother is then less important to the church than its identity and reputation and standards, or even than the power of its leaders which is threatened by the offender's not conforming.

D. *Responsibility moves from the brother or sister to the church disciplinarian;* the bishop or the deacon (in Protestantism), the priest (in Catholicism) is charged ex officio with the duty of reprimand: (1) this depersonalizes the process, for the official disciplinarian will be farther from the offense, and will be concerned to demonstrate his fairness by treating all alike; (2) this furthermore undermines the other ministries which that minister should be exercising in the church; and (3) such delegation of power by-passes the express instruction of Matthew 18:15 to the effect that the first approach made to the guilty one by anyone should be "between you and him alone," that is, such an approach should exclude any discussion with a third party.

E. *In line with these misunderstandings, there may well develop the idea of a distinction between several categories of sin.* Public and scandalous offenses (sexual sins, theft and murder) or ritual taboos (alcohol and dancing in pioneer Protestantism) can be dealt with in a depersonalized, puritan discipline. But talebearing, pride and avarice cannot. The sins of the weak and sensual are magnified; those of the proud and strong are not named. Now if the New Testament authorizes any distinction at all between the severity levels of different kinds of sin—which is challengeable—it would be the other way around.

We may sum up this constant temptation to deform the binding and loosing experience with the word *puritan.* It is this abuse which has given to terms like *discipline, admonish* and *reprove* a distasteful ring in our ears. The puritan is concerned to impose the right standards on a whole society; Jesus and the free church are concerned to see the fellow believer grow freely in the integrity with which he or she lives out the meaning of a freely made commitment to Christ.

Discussion questions on the misunderstandings of discipline.
☐ Can you illustrate from experience any of the reformations listed above?
☐ Talk back; are there any understandings, listed above as "misunderstandings," which you think are correct? Why?
☐ Can you see some other reasons for the repeated loss, with the passage of time, of the practice of fraternal discipline?
☐ Is the above outline right in rejecting the idea of "punishment"? Does society need to punish the offender? Does the offender need to feel punishment? Does the moral order call for it?

IX. Misunderstandings of the Meaning of Love
The expression of evangelical forgiveness and discernment can just as easily be lost in the reaction against puritanism, which in the name of love leaves the individual alone with his struggles, his guilt, his uncertainty, and his mistaken certainties. Once the puritanical approach has been discredited by its friends, and undermined by the pressure of the larger society (which in its demands for conformity at other points is, however, also a backhanded kind of puritanism), the undiscerning and adolescent reaction which comes most easily is that of letting every individual be his own master.
A. *This failure to intervene* may be explained (sincerely or in cowardice) in terms of "love" or "acceptance" or "respect for individual difference" or "letting him free to work it out himself." There is an element of truth in this feeling; it is understandable to the extent to which puritanism is assumed to be the only alternative. But the procedure commanded by Jesus is also an expression of "love" and "acceptance," and still "lets him work it out himself."

During the first generation of reaction against a puritanical heritage, people may have sufficient moral rigor built into their reflexes that they may seem to be able to get along with a great degree of individual autonomy, and still not loose their moorings. Yet once the backlog of puritanical certainties is no longer there to lean upon and to react against, it again becomes visible that individual freedom is a most deceptive and loose kind of conformity to the world.
B. *There is the excuse of modesty.* Who am I to say he has sinned because I too am a sinner, because I don't know his situation ("sin" is after all a relative matter) or because everyone must find his own way?

We can agree that no one knows the offender's situation quite as he does. This is why the one who reproves him must "go to him alone" instead of judging him a priori for what he is thought to have done. This approach thus safeguards all the valid concerns of what is currently advertised as "situation ethics."

It is true as well that we are all sinners; but Jesus does not let the duty to forgive depend on one's own sinlessness; he precisely says that it is those who are forgiven who must forgive.

C. *The excuse of "maturity"*: if I am emotionally strong I can forgive and forget without bothering the brother, the sister, or the church. This attitude, which can be the sincere expression of a forgiving spirit and of wholesome emotional resilience, is based on the mistaken assumption (see above, IV/E/1) that the concern of the process is for the one offended rather than for the offender.

D. *The idea of blanket forgiveness* by virtue of theological understanding or by liturgy:

1. Forms which prescribe the phrases for the routine confession of sin and the assurance of forgiveness are part of the regular liturgies of the Anglican and Lutheran communions;

2. Anyone who knows, as any Christian should know, that God is a forgiving God, can apply this knowledge to herself or himself, as a purely mental operation, and thus have the assurance of one's own reconciliation;

3. Anyone accustomed to the diluted "lay" forms of popular contemporary psychology knows that "self-acceptance" is for the contemporary person a possibility, a virtue, or even a duty. Thus, knowing it should be done and therefore must be possible, one may seek consciously to "forgive himself."

E. *The anti-Roman-Catholic argument* that forgiveness is not within the authority of the church. As at other points, some Protestants have been driven by their anti-Catholicism to become unbiblical. The medieval Catholic penitential practice involves definite abuses:

1. Limiting the forgiving function to a sacramentally authorized priest.

2. Tying it to a prescribed set of acts of penance.

3. Trying to make it consistent, legal, impersonal, impartial, so as to apply in the same way to all without favoritism (the same deformation as in puritan Protestantism).

4. Leaving room for the idea that the sin is "made right" not wholly by forgiveness but also partly by reparation or penance.

5. Linking absolution to the church hierarchy's control of the means of grace.

There is in all these abuses no reason to reject the offering of words of pardon from one believer to another.

F. *Individualism seen in its various forms:* as a modern humanist philosophy making each person a law unto himself; or as an antipuritan reaction denying that it is the business of the church to reach common decisions about contemporary faithfulness; or as a spiritualist glorification of guidance or illumination received immediately by the individual.

G. *Arguing that the church should preach about sin* or sinfulness but not deal with specific sins or specific sinners.

H. *All of the above distortions* relate to the application of reconciling concern to moral offense; the other possibility is to call into question the principle of morality itself as a common concern. Many contemporary currents of thought, within and without the church, challenge whether a common Christian moral position is attainable, or desirable, or binding.

This argument needs to be faced honestly. But for present purposes we must only recognize that it is a quite different question from the ones we have been dealing with thus far. The New Testament and Christians until modern times agreed that such moral consensus is desirable. With those who challenge this, the argument must be carried out on a different basis and a different level from the present outline.

X. Diversions and Evasions

A. *The mechanical detour.* Since as we have seen the two dimensions of discernment and forgiveness, or decision making and reconciliation, are intimately mingled, every estrangement between persons also has about it a difference in discernment: a conflict about fact, or about proper procedures or wrong policies. Differences in opinion or policy are both causes and effects of personal disharmony.

It is therefore no surprise that the "detour" of attention to mechanics is frequently resorted to. Divided about principles or persons, and unwilling to face the strain and threat of reconciliation, we concentrate instead on procedures. The prospect of loving frankness, with admonition and forgiveness flowing freely both ways, is threatening by its unfamiliarity. Ours is an age of great psychological and sociological self-awareness, which heightens the consciousness of the threat. Ours is also an age of great organizational concern, which increases our ability to find ways to avoid such an open meeting of souls.

1. There is evasion by compromise, by-passing an issue without resolving it, hoping it will resolve itself.

2. There is evasion by superior power, overcoming the other not by reconciliation but by maneuvering, by parliamentary or administrative methods.

3. There is evasion by appeal to outside authority. That authority may be an expert in sociological theory or management methods, or in theological correctness or empirical research, who is called in to provide us an answer without opening up the personal dimensions.

Calling in the outsider depersonalizes the issue. Should the outsider take "our side," this is powerful confirmation of our rightness which we can ask everyone to submit to, whatever may have been the personal feelings. Should he take "the other side," we can bow to authority with less "loss of face" than would have been involved in listening and submitting to the sister or brother.

B. *The therapy detour.* A detour is also possible by taking the matter to a counselor whose solution is felt to be preferable because it is given by a "doctor figure" rather than a sister or brother:

1. One is not otherwise personally or socially related to him; both "doctor" and "patient" deal with one another as roles rather than as persons.

2. The "doctor's" very involvement in the problem labels the trouble as "illness" rather than "blame," so that one feels less responsible.

3. The "doctor" is sure to accept me, for that is his role.

4. The "doctor" solves my problem by virtue of technical competence and not through personal commitment to me.

5. The "doctor" serves me for payment; once payment is made there is no more hold on me, and I need feel no debt of commitment to the person or gratitude.

6. I can trust the "doctor" to keep my problem confidential.

This characterization of the therapeutic counselor is not meant to be an evaluation; our only point here is that this resource is different in kind and in function from that of the community.

C. *Evasions related to an incomplete view of human nature.* In one way or another all of the misunderstandings which stand in the way of a confident and loving binding and loosing are variations on a basic misconception of human nature. If we think of ourselves as normally not in need of admonition and restoration and guidance from the brotherhood, then we think of the procedure described in Matthew 18 as exceptional, for use only in extreme cases.

1. We would hope not to have to apply it often, and then only after other means of evasion or of indirect pressure had failed.

2. We would hope, as serious, well-intentioned Christians, not to need such treatment ourselves.

3. We would withdraw from exercising this ministry to others if in need of it ourselves.

4. We would "hesitate to make an issue" of another's peculiarities, as long as they were within the limits of the tolerable.

5. We consider the need for this admonition to be itself a sign of blameworthy weakness. We tend to look down on the person who needs it and respect instead the irreproachable person. Thus we are on the way toward the puritan deformation again.

6. We see no direct connection between this matter and the gospel, since by *gospel* we mean a kind of general graciousness of God toward sinfulness in general rather than concrete forgiveness for oneself or one's sister or brother. We seek instead to fix a great gulf between divine and human forgiveness.

7. We concentrate our attention on an initial Christian experience of conversion and regeneration, or on a specific second experience of sanctification brought about by God alone. These emphases in many cases can become a denomination's special emphasis and can be identified and spoken about more easily. They may even help us to think that, following this divine work, daily forgiveness should be less necessary.

D. *Hindrances in unbelief.* Thus far, our analysis of how churches lose the reality of forgiving fellowship has assumed the best of intentions, as if misinformation were keeping Christians from doing what would otherwise be easily attained. It certainly is possible that misunderstandings and erroneous teachings can stand in the way of knowing, and thereby in the way of doing right. Yet ignorance or misinformation only complicate the problem; they do not create it. The real reason we do not go to our brother lies in disobedience; that of the individual or of the community.

The individual neither loves sufficiently nor believes sufficiently in the renewing power of the Holy Spirit, to go to the other when it is one's duty, when both the outer command and the inner awareness are clear despite all misunderstandings.

XI. The Price of the Neglect of This Function of the Church

A. *We are not faithful.* This failure to be the real church in which the Spirit works shows up in a sense of formality and unreality in the life of the congregation. More and more we have the feeling that we are going through the motions of what was meaningful in another age, and that the real depths of concern and of motivation are not touched in what we speak about when we are together.

In the absence of clear devotion to this central working of the Spirit by which the church is defined, we tend to take refuge in other good works and other manifestations of the presence of the Spirit which, although good, constructive, and proper in their place, are nevertheless not equally indispensable.

In the more "respectable" segments of Christendom these secondary works are focused in the areas of Christian nurture and social action. In the more "enthusiastic" portions of the church the concentration is on the outwardly ecstatic aspects of the Spirit's working. The concentration on the "respectable" or on the "enthusiastic" works of the Spirit (as well as the almost universally accepted assumption that the two are mutually exclusive) is but a sign of the loss of the living center in which a functioning brotherhood would hold in genuine unity the entire range of the Spirit's gifts.

B. *We are not forgiven, and we are not guided.* The widespread success of secular and sub-Christian sources of forgiveness and guidance in society (psychiatry, Peale-ism, astrology, Ann Landers and Abigail Van Buren) are testimony to the lostness of living without the forgiving and discerning resources of fellowship. Here we see the desperate and irrational lengths to which people will go to find a substitute.

C. *But the real tragedy* is not that *individuals* within the larger society are without guidance and without forgiveness; it is that as *church* we have come to respect as a sign of maturity the willingness to live with directionlessness and with unreconciled divisions and conflicts. We reject as immature or impatient those who would argue that something definitely must or must not be done.

We make a virtue of the "acceptance" of intolerable situations, rather than of the obedience in openness and forgiveness which could transform situations. Especially we have come to "live with" a situation in which, as a defense against "defenders of the faith" whose methods in the past were less than redemptive, we are satisfied with trying to do a decent job day by day without taking responsibility for the direction in which churches and their institutions are evolving. A sense of not knowing where to turn next is pervasive among denominational leaders.

D. *The church which does not forgive is not a missionary church.* A great mass of contradictory testimony springs out of the widespread recognition of the ineffectiveness of the Christian churches before their missionary task. For some, the corrective should be a renewed dedication to the forms of message and ministry found effective in other ages, in the confidence that it is adequate if preached with conviction.

For others, the message must be "translated" into another more relevant idiom in order to "communicate." For others, it is the "structure" of church activity which must change to fit the new urban world. For still others, *mission* itself must be redefined to refer to all the wholesome contributions the church makes to her society, independently of winning the allegiance of additional individuals.

These discussions are worthwhile in their own right; yet the danger is great that they become a substitute for the church's being the forgiving and discerning fellowship of which we are speaking. No juggling of vocabulary or of agencies or of times and places and forms of meeting can fill the vacuum where fellowship is missing. Yet where believers do interact in reconciling love, the tool is at hand for changing both societies and personalities.

XII. Wider Implications

This outline has intentionally been kept simple and practice-oriented, since it is on the level of simple obedience to a clear duty that we usually go astray. Yet if this task were tested by and related to broader kinds of theological meditation, or other ways of understanding and helping man, the import of what we have been discussing would be all the stronger.

A. *The human is a social being,* not by error nor by compromise but by nature and by divine intent.

After centuries of trying best to understand the person as a spirit in a hostile body or an individual in a hostile world, both theology and psychology are seeing that what one is is not separable from the network of one's social relationships. Thus healing, whether from sin or from sickness, is inseparable from the healing of human relationships.

B. *The work of God in the whole biblical story,* from Abraham to Pentecost and from Adam to the New Jerusalem, is the creation of covenant community, in which the loving relationships are the outworking of people's obedience to the reconciliation worked for them by God. Salvation is not just fishing single souls out of the mass for a privileged destiny; salvation is loving human relationships under God.

C. *The witness of the church* is not only the verbal message of public preaching; in a day of cheapened words this may become the least important language, especially for the outsider. The witness of the church always includes and may sometimes center upon the quality of personal relationships which even the outsider may observe.

D. *We may be humiliated,* but we should not be surprised, to discover that Christian duty is also secular good sense. Current techniques in institutional and industrial management, replacing hierarchical authority by group decision processes, commending frankness as more efficient than deviousness, are now recognized as good (i.e., efficient) practice.

E. *The readiness not only to forgive* but to make forgiveness the instrument and the standard of all church experience is of a piece with the broader theme of suffering servanthood, the theme which stretches from Hosea and Isaiah 42, 49, 52—53 through Christ himself to the cross-bearing of his disciples.

Forgiveness is not a generally accessible human possibility; it is the miraculous fruit of God's own bearing the cost of man's rebellion. Forgiveness among us also costs a Cross. One can go to one's brother or sister only as God came to us; not counting our trespasses against us. Forgiveness does not brush the offense off with a "think nothing of it"; it absorbs the offense in suffering love.

F. *The process of binding and loosing in the local brotherhood* provides the practical and theological foundation for the centrality of the local congregation. It is not correct to say, as some extreme Baptists and Churches of Christ do, that the local gathering of Christians can be called "the church." The Bible uses the term *church* for all of the Christians in a large city or even in a province. The concept of local congregational autonomy has therefore been misunderstood when it was held to deny mutual responsibilities between congregations or between Christians of different congregations.

We understand more clearly and correctly the priority of the congregation when we study what it is that it is to do. It is only in the local face-to-face meeting, with brethren and sisters who know one another well, that this process can take place of which Jesus says that what it has decided stands decided in heaven. Whether the outcome be the separating of fellowship or its restoration, the process is not one which can be carried on in a limited time and by means of judicial formalities; it demands conversation of a serious, patient, sustained, loving character. Only when people live together in the same city, meet together often, and know each other well, can this "bearing of one another's burdens" be carried out in a fully loving way.

The church is defined by this process; not by a legal organization nor by a purely spiritual doctrinal criterion. The church is where two or three or more are gathered in the name of Jesus around this kind of need. The synod, or the overseer from outside the congregation, may very well be of real assistance and may very well share something of the character of the "church"; but there is no way whereby such persons or mechanisms could replace the process of loving and binding fraternal conversation.

G. *If we understand deeply enough* the way in which the promise of the Holy Spirit is linked to the church's gathering to bind and loose (Mt 18:19-20) this may provide us as well with a more wholesome understanding of the use and authority of Scripture. One of the most enduring subjects of unfruitful controversy over the centuries has been whether the words of Scripture, when looked at purely as words, isolated from the context in which certain persons read them at a certain time and place, have both the clear meaning and the absolute authority of revelation.

To speak of the Bible apart from persons reading it and apart from the specific questions which those persons reading need to answer, is to do violence to the very purpose for which we have been given the Holy Scriptures. There is no such thing as an isolated word of the Bible carrying meaning in itself. It has meaning only when it is read by someone, and then only when that reader and the society in which he lives can understand the issue to which it speaks.

Thus the most complete framework in which to affirm the authority of Scripture is the context of its being read and applied by a believing people which uses its guidance to respond to concrete issues in their witness and obedience. Our attention should center not on what theoretical ideas a theologian (isolated from the church) can dissect out of the text of Scripture in order to relate them to one another in a system of thought. As the apostle Paul says, it is for teaching, reproof, correction and instruction in right behavior.

Let us therefore not be concerned, as amateur philosophers, to seek for truth "in itself," as if it were more true by its being more distant from real life. The Bible is the book of the congregation, the source of understanding and insight as, with the assistance of the same Spirit under whose guidance the apostolic church produced these texts, the congregation seeks to be the interpreter of the divine purpose in her own time and place.

XIII. Textual Fine Points

A. *The phrases "to bind," "to loose":*

The classic scholarly summary of the usage of this pair of terms in the rabbinic Judaism is provided in the (German) commentary of Strack and Billerbeck (Munich 1923, pp. 738ff. dealing with Mt 16:18f.).

In the *Theological Dictionary of the New Testament* (R. Kittel, ed., Grand Rapids, Vol. II, p. 20) Prof. Büchsel, author of a very brief article on "binding and loosing," agrees that the *halakah* meaning of moral decision making was the standard usage, yet denies that Jesus could have meant this. The denial is, however, dictated not by dictionary consideration but by Büchsel's own theology.

The article by J. Jeremias on "keys" is more helpful (*Theol. Dict.*, III, pp. 749ff.). He points out that the scribes claimed this same authority (Mt 25:13).

B. *The tense of Matthew 18:18:*

The future perfect tense twice used in this verse would be rendered literally: "What you bind on earth shall have been bound in heaven; what you loose on earth shall have been loosed in heaven."

A few interpreters have sought to restrict considerably the scope of Jesus' mandate by using the future perfect restrictively, so as to mean "You should bind on earth only what has already been bound in heaven." Their practical pastoral and theological motivation is clear; a fear lest human office-bearers speak unduly in God's name.

What "has already been bound in heaven" would be hard to know from the original context, but for the twentieth-century evangelicals who argue this point (with motivations like those cited in sections VIII-X above, especially IX/E) it probably means "what is in the Bible."

This reading has been applied only in the modern version of the New Testament, translated by Charles B. Williams and printed by Moody Press (Chicago, 1952). It was argued most fully by J. R. Mantey, "The Mistranslation of the Perfect Tense . . . ," *Journal of Biblical Literature*, Vol. 58, (1939), pp. 243 ff., and refuted convincingly by Henry J. Cadbury, "The Meaning of John 20:23, Matthew 16:19 and Matthew 18:18" (ibid., pp. 251ff.).

John H. Yoder is professor of theology at the University of Notre Dame, author of The Politics of Jesus *(Eerdmans, Grand Rapids, 1972) and of other works in the fields of church history and Christian ethics.*

Notes

Chapter 1: What Is Church Discipline?

[1]John Stott, *Confess Your Sins: The Way of Reconciliation* (Waco, Tex.: Word, 1974), p. 49.

[2]John T. McNeill, *A History of the Cure of Souls* (New York: Harper and Row, 1977), p. 96.

[3]Ibid., p. 97.

[4]John Owen, *The True Nature of a Gospel Church and Its Government*, vol. 16, *The Works of John Owen* (1689; reprint ed., London: Banner of Truth).

[5]Ken Blue, "Interpersonal Church Discipline" (M.C.S. thesis, Regent College, 1979).

Chapter 2: Barriers to Church Discipline

[1]Thom Hopler, *A World of Difference* (Downers Grove, Ill.: InterVarsity Press, 1981), p. 26.

[2]Stott, *Confess Your Sins*, pp. 48-49.

[3]Daniel E. Wray, *Biblical Church Discipline* (Edinburgh: Banner of Truth, 1978), p. 1.

[4]"Marian and the Elders," *Time*, 26 March 84, p. 70.

[5]"The War Within: An Anatomy of Lust," *Leadership*, Fall 1982, pp. 30-48.

Chapter 3: Jesus and Power

[1]James Kallas, *The Significance of the Synoptic Miracles* (Greenwich, Conn.: Seabury Press, 1961).

[2]Watchman Nee, *The Body of Christ: A Reality* (New York: Christian Fellowship Publishers, 1978), p. 48, quoted in Jerram Barrs, *Shepherds and Sheep: A Biblical View of Leading and Following* (Downers Grove, Ill.: InterVarsity Press, 1983), p. 50.
[3]Ibid.
[4]Ibid., p. 83.

Chapter 4: The Ministry of Reconciliation
[1]T. F. Torrance, *Theology in Reconciliation* (London: Geoffrey Chapman, 1975), p. 7.
[2]Blue, "Interpersonal Church Discipline," p. 33.
[3]Stanley Milgram, "Some Conditions of Obedience and Disobedience to Authority," *Human Relations* 18 (1965): 57-75.
[4]Leon Jaworski with Dick Schneider, *Crossroads* (Elgin, Ill.: David C. Cook, 1981), pp. 96-100.
[5]Ibid., p. 100.
[6]E. H. Broadbent, *The Pilgrim Church* (London: Pickering & Inglis, 1931), p. 86.
[7]Ibid., p. 173.
[8]John Howard Yoder, *Binding and Loosing*, No. 14, *Concern* (Scottsdale, Pa., 1967), pp. 13-14.

Chapter 5: The Holy, Spotless Bride
[1]Owen, *True Nature of a Gospel Church*, p. 11.
[2]John Calvin, *Institutes of the Christian Religion*, ed. John T. McNeill, trans. Ford Lewis Battles, 2 vols. (Philadelphia: Westminster Press, 1960), IV, xii, 5.

Chapter 6: Restoring the Fallen
[1]Roland Allen, *Missionary Methods: St. Paul's or Ours* (London: World Dominion Press, 1912), pp. 160-61.
[2]Owen, *True Nature of a Gospel Church*.

Chapter 8: The Matthew Passage
[1]Yoder, *Binding and Loosing*, p. 10.
[2]Allen, *Missionary Methods*, pp. 160-61.
[3]Yoder, *Binding and Loosing*, p. 2.
[4]Ibid., p. 5.

Chapter 9: The Corinthian Passages
[1]Leon Morris, *The First Epistle of Paul to the Corinthians* (Grand Rapids, Mich.: Eerdmans, 1958), p. 87.
[2]John Owen, *Sin and Temptation*, ed. James M. Houston (Portland: Multnomah Press, 1983), p. 72.
[3]Some scholars deny that the offender referred to in 2 Corinthians is the same

as the one in 1 Corinthians. The point has no practical bearing on our discussion. In both cases Paul is dealing with someone excluded from the church.

Chapter 10: The Three Steps Reconsidered
[1]Owen, *True Nature of a Gospel Church*, p. 168.

Chapter 12: The Return of the Prodigal
[1]The quoted material in this chapter is based on Robert Tyler's own words which he allowed me to use in this book. As is true elsewhere in this book, names have been changed, but the substance of the story remains unchanged.

Chapter 13: Repentance
[1]McNeill, *A History of the Cure of Souls*, pp. 270-71.
[2]Donald Guthrie, *New Testament Theology* (Downers Grove, Ill.: InterVarsity Press, 1981), pp. 514-15.
[3]Tertullian, *Adv. Marc.* ii, 24.
[4]Tertullian, *De Poenitencia*, 6; our italics.
[5]Gustav Aulen, *Christus Victor*, trans. A. G. Hebert (New York: Macmillan, 1969), pp. 4-7.

Chapter 14: Sins That Don't Go Away
[1]D. W. Goodwin et al., "Alcohol Problems in Adoptees Raised Apart from Biological Parents," *Archives of General Psychiatry* 28 (1973):238; idem 31 (1974):164-69.
[2]John White, *The Masks of Melancholy* (Downers Grove, Ill.: InterVarsity Press, 1982).

Chapter 15: Confessing Sin
[1]McNeill, *A History of the Cure of Souls*, p. 161.
[2]Calvin, *Institutes*, III, iv, 12.

Chapter 16: When Leaders Go Wrong
[1]Samuel Southard, *Pastoral Authority in Personal Relationships* (Nashville: Abingdon, 1969), pp. 111-28.
[2]Ibid.

Chapter 17: An Approach to Change
[1]Robert Culp, "In Search of a Better Way," *Leadership*, Summer 1983, pp. 42-46.

Appendix: Binding and Loosing
[1]Concerning the way the nation takes over the moral authority of the church, see John Smylie, *The Christian Church and National Ethos*, Christian Peace

Mission pamphlet, Washington, D.C., 1963.

[2]Cited here from an early draft of *Balthasar Hubmaier's Works* in preparation for publication in *Classics of the Radical Reformation*. Another translation is available in Denis Janz, ed., *The Reformation Catechisms* (New York: Edwin Meelen Press, 1982), pp. 135 ff.